The Burger Meisters

The Burger Meisters

America's Best Chefs Give Their Recipes
For America's Best Burgers Plus the Fixin's

By Marcel Desaulniers

Photography by Michael Grand

Illustrations by Jennifer S. Markson

SIMON & SCHUSTER

London   Sydney   New York   Tokyo   Toronto   Singapore

SIMON & SCHUSTER
Simon & Schuster Building
Rockefeller Center
1230 Avenue of the Americas
New York, NY 10020

A KENAN BOOK
© 1993 by Kenan Books, Inc.
Text © 1993 Marcel Desaulniers
Photographs © 1993 Michael Grand
Illustrations © Jennifer S. Markson

THE BURGER MEISTERS
America's Best Chefs Give Their Recipes For America's Best Burgers Plus the Fixin's
was prepared and produced by
Kenan Books, Inc.
15 West 26th Street
New York, NY 10010

Editor: Dana Rosen
Art Director/Designer: Jeff Batzli
Photography Director: Christopher C. Bain
Food Stylist: Roscoe Betsille
Prop Stylists: Leslie Defrancesco and Margaret Braun
Typeset by Classic Type, Inc.
Color separations by Fine Arts Repro House Co., Ltd.
Printed in Hong Kong and bound in China by Leefung-Asco Printers Ltd.

1 3 5 7 9 10 8 6 4 2

Library of Congress Cataloging in Publication Data

Desaulniers, Marcel.
    The burger meisters / by Marcel Desaulniers.
       p. cm.
    Includes bibliographical references and index.
    ISBN 0-671-86538-2 : $20.00
    1. Hamburgers. 2. Condiments. I. Title.
TX749.5.B43D47 1993
    641.6′62 -- dc20   93-13662
                                                         CIP

ISBN: 0-671-86538-2

ACKNOWLEDGMENTS

No cookbook is complete without saying thank you. Without the tireless assistance and cooperation of legions, this book would not be in print. So thank you to:

My wife, Connie, for her patience and love.

Ferdinand Metz, president of The Culinary Institute of America, for being supportive of this project and for his exemplary leadership.

The forty-seven Burger Meisters, for their creativity, their time, and their energies.

My partners, for enthusiastically supporting yet another philanthropy.

Trellis Assistant Chef Jon Pierre Peavey, my right-hand man through this whole project. J. P. served as the chief burger recipe tester for *The Burger Meisters.*

Trellis Pastry Chef John Twichell, who, as the chief bread tester, once again lent his invaluable expertise to the creation of a cookbook. (John was also chief recipe tester for *Death by Chocolate.*)

Trellis Chef Andrew O'Connell, for his friendship and never-ending hard work.

Penny Seu, that's three down!

Dell Hargis, director of Alumni Affairs at The Culinary Institute, for providing the necessary nudges.

My agent, Dan Green, for the concept and execution of *The Burger Meisters.*

Dana Rosen, my editor at Kenan Books.

All the great folks at Simon & Schuster.

Weber-Stephen Products Company—the Weber Performer Grill with Touch-n-Go Gas Ignition System is terrific.

DEDICATION

To The Culinary Institute of America,
Our Alma Mater

FOREWORD

For this book, forty-seven prominent alumni of The Culinary Institute of America, the Burger Meisters, took time away from their normal routines (an oxymoron for most chefs!) to cook up the best burgers imaginable.

How does one gather such talent? Frankly, it was easy. The minute each chef heard that the purpose was to raise funds for our alma mater (the advance as well as all royalties go directly to The Culinary Institute of America), they offered unrestrained enthusiasm.

The Culinary Institute of America, located on a cliff overlooking the east bank of the Hudson River in Hyde Park, New York, is regarded as America's center for culinary learning. An independent, not-for-profit educational facility and the only residential college in the world devoted entirely to the culinary arts, the institute has been called the Harvard of cooking schools. The institute will celebrate fifty years of culinary educational leadership in 1996.

The Culinary Institute of America
433 Albany Post Road
Hyde Park, NY 12538-1499
(800) CULINARY

Contents

In his deliciously informative *Dictionary of Food and Drink,* John Mariani, the distinguished chronicler of American foods, truly legitimized the subject of this cookbook:

> **Hamburger.** Also, "burger." A grilled, fried, or broiled patty of ground beef, usually served on a "hamburger bun" and topped with ketchup, onions, or other condiments. Hamburgers, along with hot dogs, are considered the most identifiably American of food items…. The first appearance in print of *Hamburg* was in 1903…. And soon the suffix *-burger* was attached to all sorts of other foods, such as lamb, chicken, clam…. By the 1940s the hamburger was firmly entrenched as a quintessential American dish.

The variety of recipes for burgers contained in *The Burger Meisters* only reinforces Mr. Mariani's words. Burgers are the favorite food of the hard hat on the construction project, the busy nurse on an all-night shift, the movie star on location, the executive after a few days in almost any foreign venue, and most certainly the professional chef.

I am amazed at how often food conversations with my colleagues invariably turn from what is "in" to what is personally preferred. The food most widely proclaimed as the choice away from work is a burger, and as is evidenced by the recipes that follow, American chefs have not allowed their creativity to be restrained by simply relying on a ground beef patty, a bun, and a bottle of ketchup.

Contemporary American chefs have staked a claim in culinary history by revitalizing—not reinventing—American regional foods. Likewise, their burgers have been inspired by regional and ethnic pantries as well as local lifestyles.

From Phyllis Flaherty-Bologna's New England Maple Barbecued Pork Burger, served on an Anadama Roll and accompanied by Celeriac Chips, to Carl Walker's grilled Buffalo Burger, served on a Fresh Sage Tortilla with Piquant Avocado, *The Burger Meisters* illustrates the creative, delicious, and exciting possibilities that burgers offer to the backyard grill cook as well as the professionally trained chef.

Marcel Desaulniers
Williamsburg, Virginia

Burger Prep 101

Master chefs, executive chefs, corporate chefs, chef-instructors. With this impressive group of food professionals, one would hope to find a consensus of information about burgers. We all certainly have a vast array of expertise and passion on the subject, but what we do not have are firm rules distinguishing the right way from the wrong way. Since so many variables exist when working with all foods, new and conflicting information is constantly appearing.

Burgers are like other foods in this regard. As soon as one learns that a certain method is the only method, along comes another expert touting his or her procedure. So what follows is excellent information that the next cook may choose to enhance, debunk, or run with.

INGREDIENTS

With almost no exceptions, the ingredients in this cookbook are available in most major supermarkets. Sources for some of the more esoteric ingredients, such as buffalo meat and fish sauce, are listed. But for the most part, a normal shopping excursion should allow you to gather all specified foods.

Of course, substitutions are not only allowed but encouraged. The Duck Burger, for instance, is also exceptional using dark turkey meat. Almost all of the red meats are interchangeable; use beef instead of buffalo, pork rather than veal, lamb instead of beef. The Low Country Rabbit Burger would be quite delicious using chicken. The key element with any ingredient is quality and freshness—so always buy the best available.

Because fresh herbs impart subtle and specific flavors to foods, we recommend that they be used whenever possible. Although dried herbs may be substituted when fresh herbs are not available, their intensity of flavor requires that they be used with a very light hand. Another option is to substitute a more widely available fresh herb, such as parsley, when the specified fresh herb cannot be found.

RECIPES

All the recipes submitted by the Burger Meisters were tested at least three times. First the recipes were developed and tested by the Burger Meisters in their own kitchens. These recipes were then tested and adapted for nonprofessionals by Jon Pierre Peavey and John Twichell at The Trellis Restaurant using consumer-oriented equipment. Adjustments were made, certain techniques were standardized, and then the recipes were finally tested at the home of the author, Marcel Desaulniers. Marcel cooked all the burgers and accompaniments with Jon Pierre Peavey, and all the bread, bun, and roll recipes were done with John Twichell. The results of all this testing are recipes that are easily understood and that actually work. They also taste fantastic.

MISE EN PLACE

We had to use at least one "chef" term: *mise en place,* which literally means "to put in place." This term refers to the organizational method by which most chefs operate, whereby they organize, process, partially cook, and in some cases totally prepare ingredients. This allows the cook to prepare recipes efficiently and as close as possible to the time of consumption.

In every recipe in this cookbook, the list of ingredients is the *mise en place.* Prepare the ingredients prior to assembling the recipe (for example, roast, skin, and seed the chiles) and you will have, in effect, the *mise en place.*

EQUIPMENT

As previously mentioned, all the recipes in *The Burger Meisters* were tested using consumer equipment, which means that everything needed to make the recipes is available to the home cook. Certainly, there are many enterprising people who make a living selling great gadgets that ostensibly make cooking just a step away from Nirvana. The truth is, if you have the passion for cooking, you can make do with or without just about any piece of equipment. However, certain tools do make life more enjoyable and burger-making easier.

CHARCOAL GRILL

The grill we used for recipe-testing is the Weber Performer Grill with Touch-n-Go Gas Ignition System. This kettle grill has an innovative system that allows you to light the wood or charcoal with the push of a button; a gas burner directs the flame onto the wood or charcoal, and within a few minutes you have "takeoff." Additionally, this grill has many features that make outdoor cooking essentially trouble-free. A variety of grills can be used to prepare the burgers in this book, from the widely used kettle grill to the economical and popular hibachi.

FLAT GRIDDLE

Many range manufacturers offer the option of a flat griddle. Although not essential, this is a worthwhile feature if you have a large family or entertain a great deal. The griddle offers a cooking surface that is designed to sustain high temperatures as well as accommodate a substantial amount of volume.

FOOD GRINDER

All recipes specifying "grind the food through a meat grinder fitted with a coarse grinding plate" were tested using the KitchenAid table-model electric mixer with a food grinder attachment. This sturdy piece of equipment makes this particular food chore a breeze. When grinding food, it is important to minimize heat generated by friction, and the powerful KitchenAid is designed with this consideration in mind. However, there are many other electric mixers with grinder attachments, as well as hand-operated grinders, that could also be used for grinding food.

JAPANESE TURNING SLICER

The manually operated Japanese turning slicer will cut seedless, solid-cored vegetables such as turnips, carrots, beets, and potatoes into thin, seemingly endless strands. Look for the turning slicer in Asian markets, or purchase one through one of the various cookware catalogs that you receive in the mail.

LARGE NONSTICK SAUTÉ PAN

The sauté pan is economical, is easy to handle and clean, and, more importantly, does an excellent job of conducting heat. The best is the aluminum-clad nonstick pan, which allows the cook to prepare foods with a minimum amount of fat; it can then be cleaned with a modicum of elbow grease.

Noncorrosive Container

Foods with a high acidic quality should always be stored in containers made from a noncorrosive material, such as stainless steel or glass, in order to eliminate the possibility of a chemical reaction.

Stainless Steel Bowl

Although glass, plastic, and ceramic bowls may be utilized for many of the recipes, stainless steel bowls have been specified because they are the most sanitary and safest containers available. Stainless steel also lasts a lifetime without breaking, chipping, or cracking.

Making Burgers

Grinding Food

Although this book has an eclectic and creative list of burgers, they almost always share one specific characteristic: whether made from beef, veal, chicken, duck, pork, tuna, or shrimp, the "meat" has been ground. The "meat" can be purchased and ground by the butcher, or it can be ground at home either by an electric mixer fitted with a grinder attachment or with a hand-operated grinder. The following list provides a few specifics about grinding food:

- Be certain the equipment is impeccably sanitary.
- Chill the food grinder before using, and always grind cold food. The colder the equipment and food, the less likely it is that the food will stick inside the grinder.
- Don't be a hero—always use the stomper to push the food being ground down the feed tube. Using the stomper ensures not only that all the food will be ground but also that you will retain your digits.
- Grind the food on high speed. A slow grind will likely mash the food and will affect the consistency of the burger.

- Thoroughly sanitize the equipment after every use. A good sanitizing solution consists of 1 tablespoon bleach per quart of hot water. After it has been cleaned in soapy water, dip the equipment into the sanitizing solution, and then allow it to drip-dry (do not towel-dry).

Combining and Forming the Ingredients

Ingredients should be treated gently when making burgers. The consistency and texture of a cooked burger depends, in part, on how it was treated in the preparation stages. Certainly, the ingredients should be mixed thoroughly to evenly distribute all components, but over-handling the food can result in a tough, dense burger. Using your hands is the most efficient manner in which to combine the ingredients for most burgers. Wear a pair of thin plastic gloves not only for sanitary reasons but also to prevent the combined ingredients from getting tacky. Form the burgers gently so as not to overly compact the meat. Handle gently, and the eating will be easy.

Refrigerating and Freezing

Once the burgers are made, refrigerate them until they are to be cooked, preferably within twenty-four hours of assembly. Exceptions are the three vegetarian burgers, which can be refrigerated for two to three days before cooking.

Beef burgers oxidize quickly and start losing their bright red color in a matter of hours. Freezing burgers is not recommended for the home consumer because most home freezers simply do not freeze foods quickly enough to retain quality.

COOKING BURGERS

Most of the burgers in this book are cooked over the open flame of a charcoal grill, cooked on a flat griddle, or pan-seared in a large nonstick sauté pan.

Weather conditions will probably be a factor in how you decide to cook your burgers. (Some of the burgers for this book were cooked on an outdoor grill during a February snowstorm!) Whichever method you choose, the following list provides a few helpful tips:

- **Purchasing charcoal.** Hardwood lump charcoal is the best, for it burns cleaner and with more control than briquettes. It also burns very hot, which may not be a positive factor when cooking certain burgers. If hardwood charcoal is not available, then purchase a high-quality briquette. All the grilled burgers in this book were cooked over Kingsford brand charcoal briquettes; although most chefs prefer hardwood coal, we felt that for this book it was best to use what is most readily available.

- **Starting a fire.** The best method to start a fire is with a gas start. An electric fire starter is also an efficient and safe way to get your fire glowing. Although starter fluids are commonly used, we find them to be unsatisfactory for a variety of reasons, including safety concerns and unpleasant residual odors.

- **Understanding ventilation.** Air is an important factor in starting and controlling a fire. Fire needs a sufficient draft to feed its intensity and create good heat. On the flip side, too much air causes the fire to burn too quickly, leaving you with ashes rather than glowing coals. A grill with a cover helps control the fire. Covering the grill will limit the ventilation, and the fire will slow considerably. Removing the cover or opening all the vents will cause the fire to rage. Practice makes perfect.

- **Placement of the charcoal.** The shape or structure of the coals on the charcoal grate plays a significant role in the development of the fire. Try stacking the coals in a pyramid shape; this concentrates the heat in the core of the pile and improves the chances for a successful start.

Once the coals are intensely hot in the center of the pyramid, spread them out. Then place the cooking grate over the fire (it is a good idea to leave the grate off until a few minutes before cooking; this allows for better access to the coals, and it prolongs the life of the grate).

- **Cleaning the grill.** Successful grilling depends on a clean cooking grate. Use a wire brush to remove food residue from the grate. Clean the grate with a damp towel, then wipe it with a towel that has been dipped in vegetable oil. The grate cleans easier when it is hot, so clean it immediately following cooking. Repeat the cleaning procedure just before cooking.

- **Medium wood or charcoal fire.** Most burgers should be cooked over a medium fire (turkey and pork burgers are more successfully prepared over a low fire). A medium fire is more easily observed than described, but generally speaking, a medium fire has coals that are red with gray edges. When the coals are intensely red, the fire is too hot; white coals mean the fire is on its way out.

- **Other methods of cooking.** As previously mentioned, most burgers in this book can be cooked on a flat griddle or in a large nonstick sauté pan. Although the romance and the flavor of the fire are not present, results are usually excellent and in some instances even more desirable. For example, the Salmon Burger would be a mess to grill, and others, such as the New England Maple Barbecued Pork Burger, are more easily controlled on a griddle or in a pan.

- **Searing the burgers.** The debate is ongoing about the benefits of quickly searing, and supposedly sealing in the juices of, certain meats and certain burgers. For the facts on searing, read Harold McGee's essay on the subject, "The Searing Truth," in his book *The Curious Cook.*

When it comes to burgers, there are so many variables that only personal experience seems to confirm the best method. So be brave and experiment. Just don't be foolish and get the fire too hot (I did just that on opening day of The Trellis in November 1980, setting off the fire suppressant system and almost canceling the opening festivities!).

Useful Techniques

Allowing the Dough to Rise

With many yeast-raised breads, the dough is allowed to rise until doubled in size. This procedure is called "proofing." Proofing is best accomplished in a fairly warm location (between 70°F and 80°F) away from drafts, and the specific proofing times in this book were established in such an environment. Longer proofing may be required if ambient temperatures are cooler.

Cooling Foods in an Ice-Water Bath

This quick method of cooling heated foods such as sauces and relishes involves placing the container holding the hot food into an ice-water bath. This bath may be a larger pan, a kitchen sink, or any other container that will hold sufficient ice water to reach midway up the container holding the hot food. Stir the hot food frequently so that it will cool rapidly. This procedure will not only cool food, it will also inhibit the production of food-borne bacteria.

Peeling and Seeding a Tomato

To peel and seed a tomato, first core the stem end with a sharp paring knife. Then, using the same knife, score the opposite end of the tomato by cutting a shallow X into the skin. Drop the tomato into boiling water for 30 to 60 seconds, depending upon the ripeness of the tomato (the riper the tomato, the shorter the time in the water). Retrieve the tomato from the boiling water with a slotted spoon and immediately plunge into ice water. When the tomato is cool enough to handle, remove it from the water and peel the skin away with a paring knife, starting from the X. Next, cut the peeled tomato in half horizontally. Gently squeeze each half under cool running water, allowing the water to flush away the seeds. The tomato may be stored tightly covered in the refrigerator for two to three days.

Pitting and Peeling an Avocado

To pit and peel an avocado, use a sharp knife to cut the avocado through to the seed from end to end and all the way around. Gently twist the two halves of the avocado apart. Gently twist the seed free from the avocado by inserting the heel of the blade of a heavy knife about 1/4 inch into the seed, then giving the knife a slight turn and lifting the seed away from the fruit. Peel the skin from the avocado using a thin-bladed paring knife.

Preparing Chiles and Bell Peppers

To roast, skin, and then seed chiles or peppers, begin by charring the skin completely black. Charring can be done by holding the chile or pepper by the stem over a gas flame using a pair of metal tongs, placing the chile or pepper directly onto an electric range element, or placing the chile or pepper on the grill rack—also called the cooking grate—of a charcoal or wood fire. Turn the chile or pepper frequently while charring in order to uniformly char and blister the skin. To remove the skin, rinse the charred chile or pepper under running water. Pull the stem loose. Cut the chile or pepper in half lengthwise, then rinse each half under running water to remove the seeds. The chile or pepper may now be minced, cut in strips, or whatever other preparation the recipe requires. When working with chiles, avoid unpleasant skin irritations by handling with care. Use plastic gloves or wash hands immediately following the above procedures.

The Burgers

Bistro Burger

with Marinated Plum Tomatoes, Black Olive and Sun-Dried Tomato Bread, and Shoestring Potatoes and Frizzled Onions

Makes 4 burgers

Alison Awerbuch

Corporate Executive Chef and Partner
Abigail Kirsch at Tappan Hill
Tarrytown, New York

AT THIS EXCLUSIVE CATERING FACILITY AND RESTAURANT OVERLOOKING THE HUDSON RIVER IN HISTORIC TARRYTOWN, NEW YORK, CHEF ALISON AWERBUCH DRAWS HER INSPIRATIONS FROM AN IDYLLIC LOCUS THAT MARK TWAIN ONCE CONSIDERED FOR RESIDENCE. (ALTHOUGH TWAIN PURCHASED TAPPAN HILL, HE NEVER REALIZED HIS DREAM OF LIFE ON THE HILLTOP; PERSONAL BANKRUPTCY INTERVENED, AND HE WAS FORCED TO SELL BEFORE HE COULD MOVE IN.)

ALISON CREATED THE BISTRO BURGER AT THE REQUEST OF A CELEBRITY CLIENT WHO WANTED TO SATISFY HER HUSBAND'S BIRTHDAY WISH FOR AN ENTRÉE THAT WOULD EVOKE THE FLAVORS OF HIS TWO FAVORITE FOODS—BURGERS AND PIZZA!

If the goat cheese stuffing is not to your taste, try fresh mozzarella or even a Boursin cheese. You may also wish to vary the chopped fresh herb; tarragon, for instance, would work particularly well with the sweetness of Boursin, and fresh oregano might be just the right touch with mozzarella.

---

4   **whole shallots, unpeeled**
6   **cloves garlic, unpeeled**
1   **tablespoon olive oil**
    Salt and pepper to season
1½ **pounds lean ground beef sirloin**
1   **tablespoon Dijon mustard**
1   **teaspoon salt**

2   **ounces fresh goat cheese, broken or cut into small pieces**
1   **tablespoon chopped fresh basil**
4   **teaspoons coarsely ground black pepper**
2   **ounces shaved Parmigiano-Reggianno**
4   **fresh basil leaves**

Preheat the oven to 325°F.

Cut the shallots into quarters (do not peel). Place the shallots and garlic on a baking sheet, sprinkle with the olive oil, and lightly season with salt and pepper. Cover the baking sheet with aluminum foil. Place in the oven, and roast the shallots and garlic for 30 minutes. Remove the shallots and garlic from the baking sheet, and cool for a few minutes.

Peel the shallots and garlic, then chop the pulp and place into a 5-quart stainless steel bowl. Add the ground beef, mustard, and 1 teaspoon salt. Gently but thoroughly combine the ingredients.

Gently form the ground beef mixture into eight 3-ounce, ½-inch-thick patties.

Use a metal spoon to make a small, shallow indentation in the center of 4 of the beef patties. Equally divide the goat cheese and chopped basil into the indentations, then top each with another patty and gently form into a burger, making sure to seal all open edges. Evenly sprinkle 1 teaspoon coarsely ground black pepper over each burger. Cover the burgers with plastic wrap and refrigerate until needed.

Grill the burgers over a medium wood or charcoal fire. Cook to the desired doneness: 4 to 5 minutes on each side for rare, 6 to 7 minutes on each side for medium, and 9 to 10 minutes on each side for well-done. (This burger may also be cooked on a well-seasoned flat griddle or in a large nonstick sauté pan over medium-high heat. Cook for about the same amount of time as listed for grilling.)

Toast 8 slices Black Olive and Sun-Dried Tomato Bread on the grill or griddle or in a nonstick sauté pan until golden brown, about 1 minute.

Serve the burgers on the toasted bread. Top each burger with Marinated Plum Tomatoes, shaved Parmigiano-Reggianno, and a whole basil leaf. Serve immediately with Shoestring Potatoes and Frizzled Onions.

When the warmth of the sun can be savored with every bite of a vine-ripened tomato, you are experiencing a fruit that has just recently been plucked from the garden. If the tomatoes on hand are of this quality, you may wish to dispense with the marination altogether. On the other hand, if the tomatoes are a bit firm and lacking in succulence, consider adding a splash of red raspberry wine vinegar to the marinade and allowing them to sit for several hours at room temperature before serving.

Marinated Plum Tomatoes

Yields 4 servings

4   plum tomatoes, washed, cored, cut in half, seeded, and cut into 1/4-inch pieces
2   tablespoons extra-virgin olive oil
    Salt and freshly ground black pepper to season

Thoroughly combine all the ingredients in a stainless steel bowl or another noncorrosive storage container. Cover with plastic wrap and allow to stand at room temperature for at least 1 hour before serving.

Black Olive and Sun-Dried Tomato Bread

Makes 2 loaves (sixteen ½-inch slices)

1   **tablespoon granulated sugar**
½   **cup warm water**
1½   **teaspoons active dry yeast**
½   **cup milk**
2¾   **cups all-purpose flour**
½   **cup chopped black brine-cured olives**
½   **cup grated Parmesan cheese**
⅓   **cup yellow cornmeal**
¼   **cup chopped sun-dried tomatoes**
1½   **tablespoons olive oil**
1   **tablespoon chopped fresh oregano**
     (or 1 teaspoon dried oregano)
2   **teaspoons freshly ground black pepper**
1   **teaspoon salt**
1   **teaspoon vegetable oil**

In the bowl of an electric mixer, dissolve the sugar in the warm water. Add the yeast and stir gently to dissolve. Allow the mixture to stand and foam, about 2 to 3 minutes, then add the milk.

Place the mixing bowl on an electric mixer fitted with a dough hook. On top of the yeast-and-milk mixture, add 1½ cups flour, olives, Parmesan, ¼ cup cornmeal, sun-dried tomatoes, olive oil, oregano, pepper, and salt. Combine the ingredients on low speed, then gradually add 1 additional cup flour. Once the additional flour has been added, scrape down the sides of the bowl. Mix on low speed for 45 seconds, then once again scrape down the sides of the bowl. Continue to mix on low speed until the dough begins to form into a ball, about 30 to 45 seconds. (If a table-model electric mixer is not available, follow the directions using a hand-held mixer or kneading by hand. The mixing times will increase depending upon which alternative method is used.)

Lightly flour a clean, dry work surface, using the remaining ¼ cup flour as necessary. Knead the dough on the floured work surface for 2 to 3 minutes. Cover the dough with a kitchen towel and allow to relax for 10 to 15 minutes. Once again, knead by hand on a floured work surface until the dough is smooth and elastic, about 8 to 10 minutes.

Lightly oil a stainless steel bowl with the vegetable oil. Place the kneaded dough into the bowl and wipe the bowl with the dough. Cover the bowl with a towel. Allow the dough to rise in a warm location until it has doubled in size, about 1½ hours.

Preheat the oven to 350°F.

When the dough has doubled in size, punch it down to its original size. Divide the dough into 2 equal portions. Knead each portion into a round loaf, about 4½ inches across and 2½ inches tall. Transfer the loaves to a baking sheet that has been sprinkled with the remaining cornmeal. Cover the loaves with a dry towel. Allow the loaves to rise in a warm location until doubled in size, about 45 minutes.

Remove the towel and bake the loaves for 30 to 35 minutes. To test for doneness, lightly tap the bottom of the baked loaf; a hollow sound will indicate that the bread is done. Remove the baked loaves from the baking sheet and allow to cool to room temperature before slicing.

> *Alison loves her herb garden and suggests that if you are so inclined, many other fresh herbs would also work with this bread. Basil, which is delightfully abundant during the summer, would be quite synergic in this bread, and fresh thyme would make its own delicious statement.*

Shoestring Potatoes and Frizzled Onions

Yields 4 servings

8   cups vegetable oil
5   large Idaho potatoes, peeled and covered with cold water
1/2 cup all-purpose flour
1/4 teaspoon salt
1/8 teaspoon ground white pepper
1   large onion (about 3/4 pound), peeled, cut in half, and sliced thin
    Salt and pepper to season

Heat the vegetable oil in a deep-fryer (or high-sided, heavy-duty pot) fitted with a deep-frying basket over high heat to a temperature of 330°F.

Use a mandoline or a cook's knife to cut the potatoes lengthwise into thin strips, about 1/4 inch wide and 1/4 inch thick. Place the potato strips in a colander and rinse thoroughly under cold running water until the starch has been removed from the potatoes and the water runs clear.

Use paper towels to pat the potato strips *very* dry. Remove the deep-frying basket from the deep fryer. Place no more than one-sixth the amount of the potato strips in the basket, then insert the basket in the fryer and fry the potatoes until they are a uniformly golden yellow color, about 4 minutes. (Constantly shake the deep-frying basket, or use a skimmer, to disperse the potatoes in the hot oil while frying.) Transfer the fried strips to paper towels to drain. Repeat the frying procedure until all the potatoes

have been fried, waiting 1 minute before frying each new batch to allow the oil to return to 330°F.

Increase the temperature of the oil to 360°F.

Refry the potatoes, one-third the amount at a time, until the potatoes are golden brown and crisp, about 45 to 60 seconds per batch. Drain the potatoes on paper towels. (This second frying finishes the cooking process and makes the potatoes very crispy.) Hold the refried potatoes in a 225°F oven while frying the onions.

Lower the temperature of the oil to 330°F.

Thoroughly combine the flour, 1/4 teaspoon salt, and ground white pepper. Coat the onion slices evenly and lightly with the seasoned flour. Place one-half the amount of the onions in the deep-frying basket, shake the basket gently to remove any excess flour from the onions, then insert the basket in the fryer and fry the onions until they become golden brown. Transfer the onions to paper towels to drain. Fry the remaining onions in the same manner. (Hold the first batch of fried onions in a 225°F oven while frying the remainder.)

Combine the fried shoestring potatoes and the fried onions, lightly season with salt and pepper, and serve immediately.

> *This recipe yields 4 large portions. The method to that madness will be quite obvious once you start eating Alison's addictive pairing of spuds and onions.*

Wahoo Burger
with Asian-Style Salad and Wasabi Mayonnaise

Makes 4 burgers

Benjamin Barker
Chef/Proprietor
Magnolia Grill
Durham, North Carolina

FOR MANY, THE GREAT AMERICAN DREAM IS TO HAVE ONE'S OWN BUSINESS. FOR BEN BARKER, IT WAS TRULY A DREAM COME TRUE WHEN HE OPENED THE MAGNOLIA GRILL WITH HIS WIFE, KAREN, IN 1986. (KAREN IS ALSO THE PASTRY CHEF.)

BACK IN THE REAL WORLD, WHERE DREAMS HAPPEN ONLY WITH HARD WORK, BEN HAD "PAID HIS DUES" AT TWO OF THE BEST KITCHENS IN NORTH CAROLINA: LE RESIDENCE IN CHAPEL HILL AND THE FEARINGTON HOUSE IN PITTSBORO. AT THESE ESTABLISHMENTS, HE FINE-TUNED HIS CRAFT AND DEVELOPED THE CULINARY STYLE THAT NOW MAKES HIS MAGNOLIA GRILL ONE OF THE MOST POPULAR RESTAURANTS IN THE REGION.

BEN'S ECLECTIC STYLE OF CROSS-CULTURAL COOKING IS EPITOMIZED IN HIS WAHOO BURGER RECIPE.

2 tablespoons granulated sugar
4 circles rice paper (see Note)
1½ pounds fresh wahoo fillet, cut into 1-inch pieces (or 1½ pounds ground wahoo fillet; see Note)
2 serrano chiles, stemmed, seeded, and minced (see Note)
1 tablespoon chopped fresh basil
1 tablespoon chopped fresh cilantro

Zest of 1 lime
1 teaspoon chopped fresh mint
1 teaspoon minced garlic
1 teaspoon grated fresh ginger
1 teaspoon fish sauce (see Note)
1 teaspoon salt
1 teaspoon ground white pepper
1 tablespoon peanut oil

In a 5-quart stainless steel bowl, dissolve the sugar in 2 quarts warm tap water. Soak 1 circle of rice paper in the warm water for 1 minute. Remove the rice paper and keep in between sheets of wet paper towels. Repeat the procedure until all 4 of the circles have been soaked. Hold at room temperature until needed.

If using wahoo pieces, grind through a meat grinder fitted with a coarse grinding plate into a 5-quart stainless steel bowl. Gently but thoroughly combine the ground wahoo with the serrano chiles, basil, cilantro, lime zest, mint, garlic, ginger, fish sauce, salt, and pepper.

Gently form the ground wahoo mixture into four 6-ounce, $3/4$-inch-thick burgers.

Remove the rice paper from the wet paper towels and place each burger in the center of a rice paper circle. Fold the rice paper over the burgers, forming a packet around each burger. Cover with plastic wrap and refrigerate for at least 1 hour.

Heat a large nonstick sauté pan that has been lightly brushed with the peanut oil over medium-high heat. Sear the burgers until golden brown and cooked through, about 6 to 8 minutes on each side.

Serve the burgers with Asian-Style Salad and a ramekin of Wasabi Mayonnaise.

Note: Rice paper is made from rice flour and water and can be found in Asian grocery stores. Ben recommends Erawan brand from Thailand, which contains thirty-six $8^{1}/_{2}$-inch circles per package. Primarily used for making spring rolls, rice paper gives the Wahoo Burger a wonderful crispy finish that makes a bun or a roll unnecessary.

Wahoo is one of the most prized fish available. It has a fine white flesh that belies its genus—the mackerel family. An adequate substitute for this recipe would be yellowfin tuna fillet.

If serrano chiles are not available, substitute 2 medium-size jalapeño chiles.

Asian fish sauces are very inexpensive condiments; even the best brands cost less than two dollars for a good-size bottle. Try getting a brand recommendation from your Asian grocer.

Asian-Style Salad

Yields 4 servings

¹/₄ cup peanut oil
2 tablespoons orange juice
1 teaspoon chopped fresh basil
1 teaspoon chopped fresh cilantro
1 teaspoon grated fresh ginger
1 teaspoon chopped fresh mint
1 teaspoon light soy sauce
¹/₄ teaspoon dried red pepper flakes
1 medium carrot, peeled and coarsely grated (see Note)
1 small fennel bulb, cored and sliced thin
Salt to season
1 head curly endive, cut into ³/₄-inch pieces, washed, and dried

In a stainless steel bowl, whisk together the peanut oil, orange juice, basil, cilantro, ginger, mint, soy sauce, and red pepper flakes. The dressing may be covered and refrigerated for 2 to 3 days or used immediately.

Toss the carrots and fennel with the dressing. Adjust the seasoning with salt. Portion the curly endive onto serving plates. Divide the dressed fennel-carrot mixture equally (about ¹/₄ cup per salad) over the greens and serve immediately.

Note: The carrot may be prepared by grating in a food processor fitted with a medium grating disk.

Wasabi Mayonnaise

Yields 1 cup

1 tablespoon wasabi powder (see Note)
2 tablespoons cold water
³/₄ cup mayonnaise
Juice of ¹/₂ lime
1 teaspoon minced garlic
¹/₂ teaspoon soy sauce
¹/₂ teaspoon sesame oil
¹/₂ teaspoon rice vinegar
Salt and white pepper to season

Reconstitute the wasabi powder in the cold water.

In a 3-quart stainless steel bowl, whisk together the mayonnaise, wasabi mixture, lime juice, garlic, soy sauce, sesame oil, and rice vinegar. Adjust the seasoning with salt and pepper, and whisk until smooth and thoroughly combined.

The mayonnaise will keep tightly covered in the refrigerator for 2 to 3 days.

Note: Wasabi (known as Japanese horseradish) powder is available in Asian grocery stores. Once reconstituted, it produces a very hot greenish-colored paste. If wasabi is unavailable, prepared horseradish can be substituted to taste.

Sonoma Lamb Burger
with Grilled Yukon Gold Potatoes and Radicchio and Watercress Salad

Makes 4 burgers

Elaine Bell
Chef/Owner
Elaine Bell Catering Company
Sonoma, California

ALTHOUGH SHE PURSUED A DEGREE IN FOOD SCIENCE AND NUTRITION AT HUMBOLDT STATE, IN ARCATA, CALIFORNIA, ELAINE BELL'S DESIRE FOR A MORE TACTILE RELATIONSHIP WITH FOOD LED HER TO VENTURE TO HYDE PARK, NEW YORK. THERE, AT THE CULINARY INSTITUTE OF AMERICA, HER PHILOSOPHY ON FOOD EVOLVED.

LISTEN TO ELAINE TALK ABOUT HER BURGER RECIPE, AND YOU WILL UNDERSTAND WHY HER FOOD IS SO TASTEFULLY AND INTELLIGENTLY PREPARED.

SINCE I LIVE IN ONE OF THE MOST BOUNTIFUL FOOD AND WINE AREAS IN OUR COUNTRY, SONOMA COUNTY, I WANT TO SHARE A RECIPE THAT I FEEL CAPTURES THE TRADITION OF "WINE COUNTRY CUISINE." SONOMA COUNTY FARMERS PRODUCE WONDERFUL LAMB, SUN-DRIED TOMATOES, GOAT CHEESE, FRESH HERBS, VEGETABLES, AND OLIVE OIL. THESE INGREDIENTS HAVE BECOME STAPLES IN OUR DAILY COOKING. MY LAMB BURGER COMBINES THEM INTO A TRUE SONOMA EXPERIENCE.

2 pounds fresh lamb meat from shoulder, trimmed and cut into 1-inch pieces (or 2 pounds ground lamb meat from shoulder)

1/4 cup chopped fresh Italian parsley

7 cloves garlic (3 peeled and minced)

1 tablespoon plus 1/4 teaspoon freshly ground black pepper

2 teaspoons plus 2 pinches salt

1 teaspoon olive oil

4 ounces fresh goat cheese

6 sun-dried tomatoes, coarsely chopped

1 tablespoon toasted pine nuts

2 teaspoons chopped fresh basil

1 teaspoon chopped fresh chives

1/2 cup balsamic vinegar
Salt and freshly ground black pepper to season

Preheat the oven to 350°F.

If using lamb pieces, grind through a meat grinder fitted with a coarse grinding plate into a 5-quart stainless steel bowl.

Gently but thoroughly combine the ground lamb with the chopped parsley, minced garlic, 1 tablespoon freshly ground black pepper, and 2 teaspoons salt.

Gently form the seasoned lamb into eight 4-ounce, 1-inch-thick patties. Cover the patties with plastic wrap and refrigerate until needed.

Place the 4 whole unpeeled garlic cloves on a baking sheet and sprinkle with the olive oil. Roast the garlic in the oven until lightly browned, about 20 minutes. Transfer the garlic to a small plate and place uncovered in the refrigerator to cool, about 15 minutes. Gently remove the peels from the chilled cloves of garlic.

In a stainless steel bowl, combine the goat cheese, sun-dried tomatoes, pine nuts, basil, chives, remaining ¼ teaspoon freshly ground black pepper, and remaining 2 pinches salt. Divide the mixture into 4 equal portions. Place 1 of the chilled, peeled garlic cloves into the center of each portion, and form each into a smooth, round ball.

Use a metal spoon to make a small, shallow indentation in the center of 4 of the lamb patties. Place a goat cheese ball in each indentation, top with another patty, and gently form into a 1¼-inch-thick burger, making sure to seal all open edges. Cover the burgers with plastic wrap and refrigerate until needed.

Heat the balsamic vinegar in a small saucepan over medium-high heat. Bring the vinegar to a boil, then reduce the heat and allow to simmer slowly until the vinegar has been reduced to one-fourth its original volume (2 table-spoons), about 10 minutes. Remove from the heat and allow to cool.

Just before grilling, lightly season the burgers with salt and freshly ground black pepper, and brush them with the balsamic vinegar glaze. Grill the burgers over a medium wood or charcoal fire. Cook to the desired doneness: about 4 to 5 minutes on each side for rare, 6 to 7 minutes on each side for medium, and 8 to 9 minutes on each side for well-done. (This burger may also be cooked on a well-seasoned flat griddle or in a large nonstick sauté pan over medium-high heat. Cook for about the same amount of time as listed for grilling.)

Serve the burgers with Grilled Yukon Gold Potatoes and Radicchio and Watercress Salad.

Grilled Yukon Gold Potatoes

Yields 4 servings

- 4   **medium Yukon Gold potatoes (about 2 pounds), washed**
- ¼   **cup extra-virgin olive oil**
      Salt and freshly ground black pepper to season
- 2   **tablespoons minced fresh chives**

Preheat the oven to 400°F.

Pierce the potatoes 2 or 3 times with a fork. Bake the potatoes on a baking sheet covered with aluminum foil for 50 minutes. Transfer to a dinner plate and place uncovered in the refrigerator to cool thoroughly, about 30 minutes.

Slice the chilled potatoes into ¼-inch-thick slices. The sliced potatoes may be covered with plastic wrap and refrigerated for up to 2 days before grilling.

Just before grilling, thoroughly coat the sliced Yukon Gold potatoes with the olive oil, and season with salt and pepper. Grill the potatoes over a medium wood or char coal fire until golden brown, about 3 to 5 minutes on each side. Sprinkle the potatoes with the chives and serve immediately.

> *Many other potatoes can be used in this recipe, including Idaho or Washington State baking potatoes; even red bliss potatoes would work well. No matter which variety you use, be certain to bake thoroughly and to chill the potatoes.*

Radicchio and Watercress Salad

Yields 4 servings

- 6   **tablespoons extra-virgin olive oil**
- 2   **tablespoons red wine vinegar**
- 1   **medium clove garlic, peeled and crushed**
- 1   **tablespoon chopped fresh Italian parsley**
- ½   **teaspoon cracked black pepper**
- ¼   **teaspoon salt**
- 1   **large head radicchio (about 8 ounces), cored, torn into 2-inch pieces, washed, and dried (see Note)**
- 1   **large bunch watercress, stems trimmed, washed, and dried**
- 2   **tablespoons toasted pine nuts**

In a small stainless steel bowl, whisk together the olive oil, red wine vinegar, garlic, parsley, pepper, and salt. Combine thoroughly. Cover with plastic wrap and hold at room temperature for up to 3 to 4 hours. Just before using, whisk the ingredients to thoroughly combine, and remove the garlic clove.

Place the prepared radicchio and watercress in a large bowl, and drizzle the dressing over them. Add the pine nuts. Gently toss all the ingredients together until the greens are lightly coated. Serve immediately.

Note: Radicchio's cabbagelike appearance has it frequently being mistaken for just that. Radicchio has a unique, subtle bittersweet flavor that sets it apart from cabbage—and other greens, for that matter. It can be found year-round, albeit of varying quality, in most major markets.

Chicago Beer Burger
with Beer-Braised Onions and Mushroom Beer Ketchup

Makes 4 burgers

Carlyn Berghoff
President/Owner
Carlyn Berghoff Catering
Chicago, Illinois

CARLYN BERGHOFF IS A FOURTH-GENERATION MEMBER OF ONE OF CHICAGO'S BEST-KNOWN RESTAURANT FAMILIES. HER GREAT-GRANDFATHER OPENED HIS FIRST CAFÉ AND MICRO-BREWERY THERE IN 1898, AND TO THIS DAY THE BERGHOFF NAME SIGNIFIES A WINDY CITY INSTITUTION OF HEARTY FULL-FLAVORED FOOD AND HOME-BREWED REGIONAL BEER. WITH THIS HERITAGE IN MIND, CARLYN AND EXECUTIVE CHEF DAVID NORMAN, ALSO A CULINARY INSTITUTE OF AMERICA GRADUATE, WERE INSPIRED TO CREATE A BURGER AND ACCOMPANIMENTS THAT ARE ALL TOUCHED BY THE BERGHOFF TRADITION OF COMBINING GOOD FOOD AND GOOD BEER.

For an attractive garnish, use a spray of watercress with a few sliced raw mushrooms sprinkled with lemon juice.

1½ **pounds ground beef chuck**
2 **tablespoons beer**
½ **teaspoon Tabasco Sauce**
¼ **teaspoon Worcestershire sauce**

Salt and pepper to season
4 **½-ounce slices brick cheese (see Note)**
4 **Best Burger Buns (see page 109), cut in half**

In a 5-quart stainless steel bowl, gently but thoroughly combine the ground beef, beer, Tabasco Sauce, Worcestershire sauce, and salt and pepper to season.

Gently form the seasoned beef into four 6-ounce, 1-inch-thick burgers. Cover the burgers with plastic wrap and refrigerate until needed.

Grill the burgers over a medium grill or charcoal fire. Cook to the desired doneness: 3 to 4 minutes on each side for rare, 5 to 6 minutes on each side for medium, and 8 to 9 minutes on each side for well-done. Top each burger with some of the Beer-Braised Onions and then with a slice of the brick cheese and allow it to melt. If you have a cover for the grill, quickly melt the cheese by placing the cover over the grill for a few moments. (This burger may also be cooked on a well-seasoned flat griddle or in a large nonstick sauté pan over medium-high heat. Cook for about the same amount of time as listed for grilling.)

Toast the buns, cut side down, on the grill or in a nonstick sauté pan until golden brown, about 1 minute.

Serve the burgers on the toasted buns with a ramekin of Mushroom Beer Ketchup.

Note: Uniquely Midwest American, brick cheese has a pungent quality that has been compared to a cross between a well-aged cheddar and a Limburger. If you are not able to turn up any brick cheese, don't be timid: slap on a piece of your favorite sharply flavored cheese.

Beer-Braised Onions

Yields 1 cup

1 tablespoon unsalted butter
1 large onion (about ³/₄ pound), sliced thin
1 cup beer
1 teaspoon granulated sugar
¹/₂ teaspoon salt

Melt the butter in a 3-quart saucepan over medium-high heat. Add the onions and sauté, stirring frequently, until the onions are very tender, about 5 to 6 minutes. Add ³/₄ cup beer, sugar, and salt. Cook until all the beer has been absorbed by the onions and they begin to brown lightly, about 16 to 18 minutes. Add the remaining ¹/₄ cup beer and bring to a simmer. Place on the Chicago Beer Burgers.

These onions can also be cooled and refrigerated until needed. Heat the cooled onions to a simmer before using. When the onions are hot, perk up their flavor with a splash or two of beer.

> *Try a Berghoff beer with your burger. Choose the regular, light, or dark brew, and enjoy it wherever you like, as it is available nationwide.*

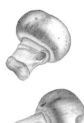

Mushroom Beer Ketchup

Yields 1 ¹/₂ cups

1 tablespoon unsalted butter
1 small onion (about ¹/₄ pound), chopped
¹/₄ pound mushrooms, stems trimmed, sliced
3 ounces beer, hot
¹/₃ cup ketchup
1 tablespoon distilled white vinegar
¹/₄ teaspoon granulated sugar
¹/₄ teaspoon salt

Melt the butter in a 3-quart saucepan over medium heat. Add the onions and sauté until tender, about 3 to 4 minutes. Add the mushrooms and sauté for an additional 3 to 4 minutes.

Remove the saucepan from the heat and add the beer, ketchup, white vinegar, sugar, and salt. Use a quick-prep hand blender to puree the mixture until smooth, or remove the mixture from the saucepan and puree in a food processor fitted with a metal blade or in a blender.

Return the saucepan with the pureed mixture to medium heat. Bring the mixture to a boil, then reduce the heat and allow to simmer until slightly thickened, about 12 minutes. Remove from the heat and cool in an ice-water bath. Transfer the Mushroom Beer Ketchup to a noncorrosive storage container and refrigerate for 24 hours before using. This ketchup will keep in the refrigerator for several days.

> *Although the Mushroom Beer Ketchup is a delightful addition to the Chicago Beer Burger, it also works well with a variety of other burgers as well as other grilled meats.*

# Plymouth Turkey Burger
with Cranberry Relish and Country-Style Mashed Potatoes

Makes 4 burgers

John Bowen
Executive Vice President
Johnson & Wales University
Providence, Rhode Island

GRADUATION FROM THE CULINARY INSTITUTE WAS JUST THE FIRST STEP IN JOHN BOWEN'S ACADEMIC INVOLVEMENT IN THE CULINARY FIELD. HE WENT ON TO COMPLETE HIS BACHELOR OF SCIENCE DEGREE AT JOHNSON & WALES UNIVERSITY, SERVED ON THE FACULTY THERE, AND LATER EARNED A MASTER'S DEGREE IN MANAGEMENT.

BEFORE ASSUMING HIS RESPONSIBILITIES AS EXECUTIVE VICE PRESIDENT, JOHN WAS THE DEAN OF THE CULINARY ARTS DIVISION OF THIS RHODE ISLAND–BASED SCHOOL.

ALTHOUGH THIS TASTEFUL LOW-FAT BURGER RECIPE WAS NOT CARRIED OVER ON THE *MAYFLOWER*, THE PILGRIM "SPIRIT" OF ITS FLAVOR IS SURE TO MAKE BURGER HISTORY.

1	tablespoon unsalted butter
1/2	cup finely diced onions
2	cloves garlic, minced
1 1/2	pounds boneless and skinless white turkey meat, cut into 1-inch pieces (or 1 1/2 pounds ground white turkey meat; see Note)
1	teaspoon salt
1/2	teaspoon ground white pepper
1/2	cup dry bread crumbs
4	Best Burger Buns (see page 109) or other favorite buns, cut in half
4	tablespoons mayonnaise Curly endive leaves, washed and dried

Heat the butter in a small nonstick sauté pan over medium heat. When the butter is hot, add the onions and garlic, and sauté until the onions are translucent, about 3 to 4 minutes. Transfer the onions and garlic to a dinner plate, and place uncovered in the refrigerator to cool.

If using turkey pieces, grind the turkey through a meat grinder fitted with a coarse grinding plate into a 5-quart stainless steel bowl.

Add the cooled onions and garlic, salt, and pepper to the ground turkey, and gently but thoroughly combine.

Gently form the turkey mixture into four 6-ounce, 1-inch-thick burgers. Cover the burgers with plastic wrap and refrigerate until needed.

Preheat the oven to 325°F.

Place the bread crumbs on a pie tin or a dinner plate. Place the turkey burgers one at a time into the bread crumbs, and gently but thoroughly coat with the crumbs.

Heat a well-seasoned flat griddle or a large nonstick sauté pan over medium-high heat. When hot, cook the burgers for 2 to 3 minutes on one side. Use a spatula to turn the burgers and to press down lightly on each one. Cook the burgers for an additional 2 to 3 minutes. Place the burgers on a baking sheet in the oven until cooked through, about 14 to 18 minutes.

Toast the buns, cut side down, on the griddle or in a nonstick sauté pan over medium-high heat until golden brown, about 1 minute.

Spread each top and bottom bun half with mayonnaise. Garnish each bottom bun half with the curly endive, then place a turkey burger on the endive. Top each burger with Cranberry Relish and the top half of the bun. Serve immediately with a side dish of Country-Style Mashed Potatoes.

Note: Although this recipe specifies white breast meat, feel free to substitute dark thigh meat or to use a combination of both. When using thigh meat, be certain to remove all the skin and tendons before grinding.

Cranberry Relish

Yields 2 cups

1	Red Delicious apple
2	cups fresh or frozen whole cranberries
1	navel orange, peeled and divided into sections
1/2	cup tightly packed light brown sugar
1/4	cup pure honey
	Pinch ground cinnamon
	Pinch ground white pepper

Peel, quarter, and core the apple. Immediately place the apple pieces and remaining ingredients in a food processor fitted with a metal blade, and pulse for 5 to 8 seconds.

Heat the processed mixture in a 2½-quart stainless steel saucepan over medium-high heat. Bring the mixture to a boil, then adjust the heat and allow to simmer for 3 to 4 minutes, stirring frequently. Remove from the heat and cool in an ice-water bath. Transfer the cooled relish to a noncorrosive storage container and refrigerate tightly covered for at least 24 hours before using. The relish will keep in the refrigerator for several days.

> *For textural interest, consider adding ½ cup chopped walnuts to the cooled relish.*

Country-Style Mashed Potatoes

Yields 4 cups

2	pounds potatoes
1	tablespoon salt
8	tablespoons unsalted butter
1/4	cup milk, hot
	Salt and freshly ground black pepper to season

Wash half the amount of potatoes, then cut them into 1-inch pieces (these potatoes will be cooked with skins on). Peel the remaining potatoes and cut into 1-inch pieces.

Place the potatoes in a 4-quart saucepan. Cover with cold water and add 1 tablespoon salt. Heat the water to a boil over high heat, then lower the heat to medium and allow the potatoes to simmer until cooked through, about 30 minutes.

Drain the cooked potatoes in a colander, then place in a stainless steel bowl. Add the butter, milk, and salt and pepper to season. Mash the potatoes with a potato masher or a slotted spoon.

> *A totally indulgent and delicious substitution would be to replace the milk with heavy cream.*

Grilled Turkey Burger
with Fresh Tomato Sauce

Makes 4 burgers

Lyde Buchtenkirch-Biscardi
Team Leader for Curriculum
The Culinary Institute of America
Hyde Park, New York

EDUCATION HAS BEEN THE FOCUS OF LYDE BUCHTENKIRCH-BISCARDI'S CAREER SINCE SHE GRADUATED FROM THE CULINARY INSTITUTE OF AMERICA. FOR SEVERAL YEARS, SHE SERVED AS A CHEF-INSTRUCTOR IN THE CULINARY ARTS DIVISION AT JOHNSON & WALES UNIVERSITY IN PROVIDENCE, RHODE ISLAND. IN 1978, SHE RETURNED TO THE CULINARY INSTITUTE AND HAS SINCE MADE SIGNIFICANT CONTRIBUTIONS TO THE SCHOOL.

LYDE'S IMPRESSIVE ARRAY OF PROFESSIONAL AWARDS AND ACHIEVEMENTS INCLUDES HER DESIGNATION AS THE FIRST AND ONLY WOMAN TO BE CERTIFIED A MASTER CHEF BY THE AMERICAN CULINARY FEDERATION.

THE ITALIANATE TWIST TO LYDE'S BURGER WILL HAVE YOU SAYING *CIAO* TO OTHER TEMPTATIONS.

5 tablespoons extra-virgin olive oil
1 teaspoon minced garlic
1 teaspoon chopped fennel seeds
1½ pounds boneless and skinless white turkey meat, cut into 1-inch pieces (or 1½ pounds ground white turkey meat)
¼ cup grated fresh Parmesan cheese
1 teaspoon chopped fresh oregano
Salt and pepper to season
8 slices Focaccia (see page 82)
4 1-ounce slices mozzarella cheese

Heat 1 tablespoon olive oil in a small nonstick sauté pan over medium-high heat. When hot, add the garlic and fennel seeds, and sauté for 1 minute. Transfer mixture to a dinner plate and place uncovered in the refrigerator to cool.

If using turkey pieces, grind the turkey through a meat grinder fitted with a coarse grinding plate into a 5-quart stainless steel bowl.

Gently but thoroughly combine the ground turkey with the cooled garlic mixture, Parmesan, and oregano. Season with salt and pepper.

Form the ground turkey mixture into four 6-ounce, 1-inch-thick burgers. Cover the burgers with plastic wrap and refrigerate until needed, at least 30 minutes.

Preheat the oven to 375°F.

Prior to grilling, brush the burgers with 2 tablespoons olive oil. Lightly season with salt and pepper.

Lyde suggests accompanying her burger with marinated vegetables. Check out Sanford D'Amato's Marinated Cauliflower Salad (see page 51)—Lyde and Sanford must have been talking!

Grill the burgers over a low wood or charcoal fire. Cook for 3 minutes on each side. Remove the burgers from the grill and place on a baking sheet. (This burger may also be cooked on a well-seasoned flat griddle or in a large non-stick sauté pan over medium heat. Cook for about the same amount of time as listed for grilling.)

Brush the Focaccia slices with the remaining 2 tablespoons olive oil. Toast the Focaccia slices, oil side down, on the grill or griddle or in a nonstick sauté pan until golden brown, about 1 minute. Remove the Focaccia from the grill, and hold warm or at room temperature while finishing the burgers.

Top the burgers with Fresh Tomato Sauce. Cover with aluminum foil and place in the oven until cooked and heated through, about 10 to 12 minutes. Remove the burgers from the baking sheet and the foil. Top each burger with a slice of the mozzarella. Return to the oven for a few moments until the cheese begins to melt.

Serve the burgers on the grilled Focaccia.

Fresh Tomato Sauce

Yields 4 servings

1   tablespoon extra-virgin olive oil
1   cup diced onions
1   teaspoon minced garlic
    Salt and pepper to season
2   tablespoons sweet Marsala wine
2   large tomatoes, peeled, seeded, and chopped
2   tablespoons chopped fresh basil
1   tablespoon chopped fresh parsley

Heat the olive oil in a medium nonstick sauté pan over medium-high heat. When hot, add the onions and garlic; lightly season with salt and pepper, and sauté for 3 to 4 minutes. Add the Marsala wine and continue cooking until the Marsala has almost completely evaporated, about 2 to 3 minutes.

Add the tomatoes, lightly season with salt and pepper, reduce the heat to medium, and continue cooking until the sauce is thickened, about 15 minutes. Stir in the basil and parsley. Adjust the seasoning with salt and pepper, and serve.

The sauce can be kept warm in a double boiler for up to 45 minutes before serving. The sauce may also be cooled in an ice-water bath, then stored tightly covered in a noncorrosive container for 2 to 3 days. Reheat the sauce over medium heat.

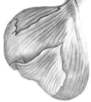

You can use other fresh herbs for this recipe as available, such as tarragon, chervil, summer savory, marjoram, or oregano.

Shepherd's Pie Burger

with Virgin-Whipped Potatoes and Country-Style Vegetables

Makes 4 burgers

David Burke
Chef/Owner
Park Avenue Cafe
New York, New York

UPON GRADUATION FROM THE CULINARY INSTITUTE OF AMERICA IN 1982, DAVID BURKE CHARTED A PERIPATETIC COURSE THAT LANDED HIM IN SOME OF THE FINEST KITCHENS IN THE UNITED STATES AND EUROPE.

THE RECIPIENT OF NUMEROUS AWARDS AND HONORS, DAVID WON THE MEILLEUR OUVRIERS DE FRANCE DIPLOMA AT THE INTERNATIONAL FOOD FESTIVAL HELD IN TOKYO IN 1988. AT THE SAME COMPETITION, HE WAS PRESENTED WITH THE NIPPON AWARD OF EXCELLENCE BY THE JAPANESE GOVERNMENT.

A SELF-CONFESSED ICONOCLAST, DAVID BURKE ENJOYS EXPERIMENTING WITH FOOD. INFLUENCED BY HIS INTERNATIONAL EXPERIENCE, HE HAS DEVELOPED A FLAIR FOR TRANSLATING CLASSIC FOREIGN CUISINES INTO UNIQUELY AMERICAN CREATIONS. ONE MIGHT SAY THAT HE HAS INDEED PUSHED THE ENVELOPE WITH HIS SHEPHERD'S PIE BURGER. ONE BITE, HOWEVER, SHOULD HAVE YOU FLOCKING TO HIS RESTAURANT.

3 large Idaho potatoes, scrubbed but not peeled

1¼ pounds trimmed venison from shoulder or leg, cut into 1-inch pieces (or 1¼ pounds ground trimmed venison from shoulder or leg; see Note)

4 slices bacon, finely chopped

2 teaspoons freshly ground juniper berries

1 teaspoon kosher salt

½ teaspoon freshly ground black pepper

1 cup vegetable oil

Trim the ends of the unpeeled potatoes so that they are flat. Cut the potatoes, one at a time, into long, thin strands on a Japanese turning slicer fitted with a medium-tooth blade. Immediately place the potato strands in cold water.

If using venison pieces, grind through a meat grinder fitted with a coarse grinding plate into a 5-quart stainless steel bowl.

Add the bacon, juniper berries, salt, and pepper to the ground venison. Gently but thoroughly combine the ingredients.

Gently form the ground venison mixture into four 5-ounce, ¾-inch-thick burgers. Cover the burgers with plastic wrap and refrigerate until needed.

Drain the potatoes. Remove any excess moisture from the potatoes by patting them dry with paper towels. Divide the potatoes into 4 equal portions, forming each portion into a small nest. Place a burger in the center of each nest. Bring the edges of the nest toward the center to completely envelop the burger (which looks a bit like the top of Medusa's head at this point). Use your hands to slightly press the potatoes into the burger.

Heat ½ cup vegetable oil in each of 2 large nonstick sauté pans over high heat. When hot, pan-fry the burgers, 2 in each pan, until the potatoes are golden brown, about 6 to 8 minutes on each side. At this point, the burgers will be rare to medium-rare; if you desire a more well-done burger, place the burgers on a baking sheet in a preheated 400°F oven for 3 to 4 minutes for medium and 6 to 7 minutes for well-done.

Place each burger on a dinner plate. Top each with hot Virgin-Whipped Potatoes and Country-Style Vegetables, allowing the vegetables to flow down onto the plate. Serve immediately.

Note: If venison is not part of your larder, you may substitute beef.

Virgin-Whipped Potatoes

Yields 4 servings

4 medium Idaho potatoes
1 tablespoon salt
1 cup milk, hot
1/2 cup extra-virgin olive oil
Salt and pepper to season

Peel the potatoes.

Place the potatoes in a 6-quart saucepan with 2 quarts water and 1 tablespoon salt. Bring to a boil over high heat. Lower the heat to medium-high, and simmer until cooked through, about 30 to 35 minutes. Drain the water from the potatoes. Whip the potatoes with the milk and olive oil until smooth in the bowl of an electric mixer fitted with a balloon whip or in a large stainless steel bowl using a wire whisk. Adjust the seasoning with salt and pepper. The potatoes may be served immediately or held warm in a double boiler for up to 1 hour.

Country-Style Vegetables

Yields 4 servings

1 1/2 cups peeled pearl onions (about 16)
1 medium carrot, cut in half and sliced thin diagonally
1 rutabaga, cut into strips 3 inches long and 1/4 inch thick
1 turnip, cut into strips 2 inches long and 1/4 inch thick
1 cup shelled green peas
2 tablespoons extra-virgin olive oil
2 tablespoons water
Salt and pepper to season
2 tablespoons chopped fresh parsley

Heat 3 quarts lightly salted water in a 5- or 6-quart saucepan. Bring to a boil. Drop the pearl onions into the boiling water and cook for 2 minutes. Add the carrots and cook for an additional 2 minutes. Add the rutabagas and turnips, and cook for 5 minutes. Add the peas and cook for 1 minute. Drain the vegetables, then plunge into ice water. When the vegetables are cooled, remove from the ice water and drain well.

At this point, the vegetables may be stored tightly covered in the refrigerator for up to 2 days.

To serve, heat the olive oil and 2 tablespoons water in a large nonstick sauté pan over medium-high heat. When hot, add the vegetables, lightly season with salt and pepper, and sauté until hot throughout, about 4 to 5 minutes. Add the parsley and toss to combine. Serve immediately.

Missouri Sirloin and Blue Cheese Burger
with Spiced Tomato Relish and Cornmeal Black Pepper Bread

Makes 4 burgers

Bill Cardwell
Chef/Owner
Cardwell's
St. Louis, Missouri

THE COMBINATION OF FLAVORS AND TEXTURES THAT CHEF BILL CARDWELL SERVES UP IN HIS MISSOURI BURGER IS JUST THE KIND OF PALATE-INVIGORATING EXPERIENCE YOU CAN LOOK FORWARD TO AT HIS EPONYMOUS RESTAURANT IN ST. LOUIS. SINCE GRADUATING FROM THE CULINARY INSTITUTE OF AMERICA, CHEF CARDWELL HAS MADE A CAREER OF CREATING FOOD WITH BROAD APPEAL. FOR SEVERAL YEARS, HE WAS THE CORPORATE EXECUTIVE CHEF FOR A CONGLOMERATE THAT GAVE AMERICA THE LIKES OF HOULIHAN'S, THE BRISTOL GRILL, AND FEDORA. NOW THE ENTERPRISING CHEF CAN BE FOUND DIRECTING HIS OWN FORTUNES, COOKING MEALS THAT HAVE HAD THE FOOD COGNOSCENTI OF ST. LOUIS BUZZING SINCE CARDWELL'S OPENED ITS DOORS IN 1986.

> *Bill suggests his favorite regional beer to enjoy with the Missouri Sirloin and Blue Cheese Burger—Millstream wheat beer, brewed in Amana, Iowa.*

1½ **pounds lean ground beef sirloin**
1 **ounce blue cheese**
   Salt and pepper to season
4 **tablespoons unsalted butter, softened**
4 **1-ounce slices white cheddar cheese**
8 **crisp slices smoked bacon**

Gently form the ground beef into eight 3-ounce, ½-inch-thick patties.

Use a metal spoon to make a small, shallow indentation in the center of 4 of the beef patties. Divide the blue cheese into four ¼-ounce portions, and form the blue cheese into smooth, round balls. Place a blue cheese ball in each indentation. Top each with another patty, and gently form into burgers, making sure to seal all open edges. Season each burger with salt and pepper. Cover the burgers with plastic wrap and refrigerate until needed.

Grill the burgers over a medium wood or charcoal fire. Cook to the desired doneness: 4 to 5 minutes on each side for rare, 6 to 7 minutes on each side for medium, and 9 to 10 minutes on each side for well-done. (This burger may also be cooked on a well-seasoned flat griddle or in a large nonstick sauté pan over medium-high heat. Cook for about the same amount of time as listed for grilling.)

Toast 8 slices of Cornmeal Black Pepper Bread on the grill or griddle or in a nonstick sauté pan for 10 to 15 seconds on each side.

Serve the burgers on the toasted bread, which has been spread with the softened butter. Top each burger with 1 slice of the cheddar, 2 slices of the bacon, and 1 tablespoon Spiced Tomato Relish. Serve immediately, accompanied by additional Spiced Tomato Relish.

Spiced Tomato Relish

Yields 5 cups

5   medium tomatoes (about 2 pounds), peeled, seeded, and chopped
1½ cups minced red onions
½   cup red wine vinegar
½   cup tightly packed light brown sugar
½   cup light Karo syrup
6   tablespoons tomato paste
1   small jalapeño chile, minced with seeds
1   clove garlic, finely minced
½   tablespoon minced fresh ginger
1   teaspoon salt
½   teaspoon ground white pepper
½   teaspoon ground cinnamon
¼   teaspoon ground mace
⅛   teaspoon ground cloves
1   tablespoon chopped fresh mint

Heat all the ingredients, with the exception of the mint, in a 3-quart stainless steel saucepan over medium-high heat. Bring to a boil, then lower the heat and simmer for 1 hour, stirring frequently. Remove the pan from the heat.

Transfer the relish to a stainless steel bowl. Cool in an ice-water bath until cold. When the relish is cold, add the mint and thoroughly combine.

Refrigerate the relish in a stainless steel or another non-corrosive container for at least 24 hours before serving.

The quantity of relish produced by this recipe is more than enough to accompany the sirloin burgers. Any remaining relish will keep tightly covered in the refrigerator for several days.

> *This relish is not only an excellent burger condiment, it also enhances such grilled meats as pork and chicken.*

Cornmeal Black Pepper Bread

Makes 1 loaf (sixteen 1/2-inch slices)

2 tablespoons honey
2 teaspoons active dry yeast
1/4 cup tap water, hot (about 120°F)
2 1/2 cups all-purpose flour
2/3 cup plus 2 tablespoons buttermilk
1/2 cup plus 1 teaspoon yellow cornmeal
1 tablespoon plus 1 teaspoon vegetable oil
2 teaspoons salt
2 teaspoons freshly cracked black pepper
1 large egg yolk

In the bowl of an electric mixer, place the honey and yeast in the hot water and stir gently to dissolve. Allow the mixture to stand and foam for 10 minutes.

Place the mixing bowl on an electric mixer fitted with a dough hook. On top of the honey-yeast mixture, add 2 1/4 cups flour, 2/3 cup buttermilk, 1/2 cup cornmeal, 1 tablespoon vegetable oil, salt, and pepper. Mix on medium speed for 2 minutes, then scrape down the sides of the bowl. Continue to mix on medium speed until the dough forms a ball, about 3 to 3 1/2 minutes. (If a table model electric mixer is not available, follow the directions using a hand-held mixer or kneading by hand. The mixing times will increase depending upon which alternative method is used.)

Coat the inside of a stainless steel bowl with the remaining teaspoon vegetable oil. Place the dough in the bowl, and wipe the bowl with the dough. Cover the bowl with plastic wrap. Allow the dough to rise in a warm location until it has doubled in volume, about 1 1/2 hours.

Flatten the dough into an 8- by 10-inch rectangle on a clean, dry, lightly floured work surface, using the remaining 1/4 cup flour as necessary. Tightly roll the flattened dough into a 2 1/2-inch-high by 10-inch-long loaf. Transfer the loaf to a baking sheet that has been sprinkled with the remaining teaspoon cornmeal. Loosely cover the loaf with plastic wrap. Allow the loaf to rise in a warm location until doubled in size, about 45 minutes.

Preheat the oven to 350°F.

Whisk the remaining 2 tablespoons buttermilk with the egg yolk, then lightly brush the top of the loaf with this egg wash. Use a sharp knife or a razor blade to make 3 diagonal, evenly spaced, 1/4-inch-deep cuts on the surface of the loaf.

Bake the loaf for 30 to 35 minutes. To test for doneness, lightly tap the bottom of the baked loaf; a hollow sound will indicate that the bread is done. Remove the baked loaf from the baking sheet and allow to cool to room temperature before slicing.

There is something very Italianate about this bread; both the taste and texture remind one of polenta. Try basting the sliced bread with olive oil and fresh chopped herbs, then grilling over a wood fire. The smell and taste may well suggest that you have arrived in Apulia!

Vegetable Pan Burger
with Roasted Garlic Paste

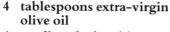

Makes 4 burgers

Michael Chiarello
Chef/Owner
Tra Vigne
St. Helena, California

GROWING UP IN A HOME WHERE EVERYTHING CENTERED AROUND THE TABLE AND THE GARDEN NATURALLY ATTRACTED MICHAEL CHIARELLO TO A CAREER IN COOKING. MANY OF HIS FAMILY MEMBERS MADE A LIVING AS BUTCHERS OR RANCHERS, AND MICHAEL FOLLOWED SUIT BY WORKING IN RESTAURANTS FROM THE AGE OF FOURTEEN AND THEN ATTENDING AND GRADUATING FROM THE CULINARY INSTITUTE OF AMERICA.

SINCE 1987, MICHAEL HAS BEEN THE CHEF/OWNER OF THE CRITICALLY ACCLAIMED TRA VIGNE IN ST. HELENA, CALIFORNIA.

AT TRA VIGNE, MICHAEL AND HIS YOUNG CREW PRODUCE THEIR OWN ITALIAN-INSPIRED DISHES FEATURING SUCH INGREDIENTS AS PROSCIUTTO, BRESAOLA, SALAMI, AND CURED OLIVES. AND IN ADDITION TO OPERATING THE VERY BUSY RESTAURANT, THERE IS A GARDEN TO TEND AND OLIVE OIL TO PRODUCE.

MICHAEL'S BURGER WAS INSPIRED BY A SOUTHERN ITALIAN DISH HIS FAMILY OFTEN ENJOYED.

4 tablespoons extra-virgin olive oil

1 medium leek, white part only, cut into thin strips 2½ inches long

1 teaspoon minced garlic

½ pound fresh wild mushrooms, stems trimmed or removed as necessary, sliced (see Note) Salt and freshly ground black pepper to season

1 tomato, peeled, seeded, and chopped

1 cup shelled green peas, blanched

1 red bell pepper, roasted, skinned, seeded, and cut into thin strips

6 spinach leaves, stemmed, washed, dried, and cut into thin strips

2 tablespoons coarsely chopped fresh basil

1 teaspoon chopped fresh thyme

½ cup dry bread crumbs

½ cup grated Parmesan cheese

4 slices Focaccia (see page 82)

4 1-ounce slices fontina cheese

Heat the olive oil in a large nonstick sauté pan over medium heat. When hot, add the leeks and garlic, and sauté for 1 minute. Increase the heat to medium-high, add the wild mushrooms, lightly season with salt and pepper, and sauté for 4 to 5 minutes. Add the tomatoes, lightly season with salt and pepper, and continue cooking until most of the liquid has evaporated, about 2 minutes. Add the peas, red bell peppers, spinach, basil, and thyme. Stir constantly until heated through, about 2 minutes. Remove the vegetables to a 5-quart stainless steel bowl, and stir in the bread crumbs and Parmesan. Adjust the seasoning with salt and pepper. Allow the mixture to cool to room temperature.

Preheat the oven to 375°F.

Gently form the vegetable mixture into four 6-ounce, 1-inch-thick burgers. Cover the burgers with plastic wrap and refrigerate until needed.

Toast the Focaccia slices in the oven for 2 minutes. Spread the cut side of the Focaccia slices with Roasted Garlic Paste. Place a vegetable burger on each slice of Focaccia. Place the burgers on a baking sheet, and top each burger with a slice of the fontina. Bake until the cheese has melted and begins to brown and the burgers are heated through, about 16 to 18 minutes. Remove the burgers and Focaccia from the oven and serve immediately.

Note: If fresh wild mushrooms are not available, an excellent substitution would be fresh shiitake mushrooms. Although these mushrooms are cultivated, they have a wonderful earthy flavor. Two ounces dried shiitake mushrooms that have been rehydrated in 1 quart warm water for 1 hour could also be used. Drain thoroughly before using.

Roasted Garlic Paste

Yields 4 servings

1   **large head garlic**
    Salt and pepper to season
2   **sprigs fresh thyme**
2   **tablespoons extra-virgin olive oil**

Preheat the oven to 325°F.

Cut ½ inch off the top of the head of garlic, exposing the cloves. Place the head in a small baking dish, and lightly season with salt and pepper. Top the head with the sprigs of fresh thyme, and drizzle with the olive oil. Cover the dish tightly with aluminum foil, and bake until the cloves are very tender, about 40 minutes. Remove the garlic from the oven and allow to cool uncovered in the olive oil for at least 1 hour at room temperature.

When cool, gently separate the cloves. Squeeze the garlic pulp out of the cloves into a small, noncorrosive bowl. Use a fork to mash the garlic pulp into a rough, textured paste. Use immediately, or keep tightly covered in the refrigerator for up to several days.

Solon Burger
with Fresh Herb Cheese and Vegetable Slaw

Makes 4 burgers

Richard Czack

*Executive Assistant to the Vice President
of Education
The Culinary Institute of America
Hyde Park, New York*

BEGINNING WITH HIS EXPERIENCE IN A
BAKERY IN HIS HOMETOWN OF CLEVELAND,
RICHARD CZACK HAS MADE A CAREER OF
STRIVING FOR EXCELLENCE. HE BUILT HIS
SKILLS IN THE MILITARY AND THEN AS A
STUDENT AT THE CULINARY INSTITUTE OF
AMERICA, WHERE HE GRADUATED WITH
TOP HONORS.

RICHARD'S INVOLVEMENT WITH THE
INSTITUTE AND HIS ACCRUEMENT OF
HONORS HAVE CONTINUED. HE JOINED
THE INSTITUTE'S FACULTY IN 1970 AND,
AFTER YEARS OF BEING A CHEF-
INSTRUCTOR, HE NOW SERVES AS
EXECUTIVE ASSISTANT TO THE VICE
PRESIDENT OF EDUCATION. IN 1988,
RICHARD WAS CERTIFIED A MASTER CHEF,
ONE OF FEWER THAN ONE HUNDRED IN
THE UNITED STATES.

RICHARD HAS NOT FORGOTTEN HIS OHIO
ROOTS, AND HIS SOLON BURGER IS NAMED
FOR A CITY THAT HE USED TO CALL HOME
IN THAT MIDWESTERN STATE.

1	tablespoon olive oil	
2	tablespoons minced onions	
1	pound ground beef sirloin	
8	ounces ground veal	

Salt and white pepper
to season

4 Best Burger Buns (see page
109), cut in half

Heat the olive oil in a small sauté pan over medium heat. When hot, add the onions and sauté lightly until translucent, about 3 minutes. Transfer the onions to a dinner plate, and place uncovered in the refrigerator to cool.

In a 5-quart stainless steel bowl, gently but thoroughly combine the chilled onions with the ground beef and ground veal. Season with salt and pepper.

Gently form the meat mixture into four 6-ounce, 1-inch-thick burgers. Cover the burgers with plastic wrap, and refrigerate until needed.

Grill the burgers over a medium wood or charcoal fire. Cook to the desired doneness: 5 minutes on each side for medium-rare, 6 to 7 minutes on each side for medium, and 8 to 9 minutes on each side for well-done. (This burger may also be cooked on a well-seasoned flat griddle or in a large nonstick sauté pan over medium-high heat. Cook for about the same amount of time as listed for grilling.)

Remove the burgers from the grill, and top each with a 1-ounce slice of Fresh Herb Cheese.

Toast the buns, cut side down, on the grill or griddle or in a nonstick sauté pan until golden brown, about 1 minute. Serve the burgers on the toasted buns accompanied by Chef Czack's vivid and crunchy Vegetable Slaw.

Fresh Herb Cheese

Yields 4 servings

- 4 ounces cream cheese, softened
- 1 tablespoon sour cream
- 1/2 teaspoon finely chopped fresh chervil
- 1/2 teaspoon finely chopped fresh chives
- 1/2 teaspoon finely chopped fresh dill
- 1/2 teaspoon finely chopped fresh parsley
- 1/2 teaspoon finely chopped fresh thyme

Place the softened cream cheese in a 3-quart stainless steel bowl, and add the remaining ingredients. Use a rubber spatula to blend the ingredients until smooth.

Place the cheese on plastic wrap or waxed paper, and roll into a solid, uniformly round tube shape approximately 1 3/4 inches in diameter.

Place the herb cheese in the freezer until firm but not frozen solid, about 1 hour. Remove the plastic wrap or waxed paper, and cut the cheese into 4 slices approximately 1 ounce each. Cover and refrigerate until needed.

Vegetable Slaw

Yields 4 servings

- 1/4 cup white wine vinegar
- 2 tablespoons granulated sugar
- 1/4 cup vegetable oil
  Salt and pepper to season
- 1 cup shredded red cabbage
- 1 cup shredded white cabbage
- 1/2 cup julienned carrots
- 1/2 cup julienned green peppers
- 1/2 cup julienned red peppers
- 1/2 cup thinly sliced red onions
- 2 scallions, trimmed and sliced thin
- 1 tablespoon minced fresh chives
- 1 tablespoon chopped fresh parsley
- 1/2 teaspoon celery seeds

In a large stainless steel bowl, whisk together the white wine vinegar and sugar. Continue to whisk until the sugar is dissolved. Then whisk in a slow, steady stream of the vegetable oil. Adjust the seasoning with salt and pepper, and combine thoroughly. Add the remaining ingredients, and toss gently to combine. Cover the bowl with plastic wrap and refrigerate for 2 hours before serving. The slaw may be kept refrigerated for 2 to 3 days.

This colorful ensemble of fresh vegetables is perfect picnic food. Not only is it a great accompaniment to Richard Czack's Solon Burger, it's also the ideal pairing with fried chicken.

Blues Burger

with Quick Barbecue Sauce, Sautéed Mushrooms, and Cheese Fries

Makes 4 burgers

Edward Daggers
Executive Chef
Kingsmill Resort
Williamsburg, Virginia

WORKING IN FOUR- AND FIVE-STAR RESORTS HAS NOT MADE EDWARD DAGGERS FORGET THE AMERICAN LOVE AFFAIR WITH BURGERS. ED HAS WON SEVERAL AWARDS IN CULINARY SHOWS, AND HIS ABILITIES IN ICE CARVING AND FOOD DECORATION HAVE GARNERED HIM REGIONAL RENOWN. BUT WHEN IT GETS RIGHT DOWN TO THE BASICS, AND WHEN YOU ARE THE CHEF AT THE RESORT THAT HOSTS THE ANHEUSER BUSCH GOLF CLASSIC, YOUR SKILLS MUST INCLUDE THE ABILITY TO PREPARE WITH ENTHUSIASM AND CREATIVITY FOODS SUCH AS HAMBURGERS.

ED DAGGERS' RECIPE IS SURE TO HAVE YOU FANTASIZING ABOUT BURGERS.

Handmade Maytag blue cheese is truly one of the world's great cheeses. For information or the location of the nearest cheese or specialty shop that sells this highly acclaimed cheese, call (800) 247-2458.

1½ pounds ground beef sirloin	Pinch cayenne pepper
½ teaspoon cumin	2 ounces Maytag blue cheese or other favorite blue cheese
½ teaspoon paprika	Salt and pepper to season
¼ teaspoon freshly ground black pepper	4 Onion Rolls (see page 89), cut in half
¼ teaspoon chili powder	
¼ teaspoon salt	

In a 5-quart stainless steel bowl, gently but thoroughly combine the ground beef, cumin, paprika, freshly ground black pepper, chili powder, ¼ teaspoon salt, and cayenne pepper.

Gently form the seasoned beef into eight 3-ounce, ½-inch thick patties. Use a metal spoon to make a small, shallow indentation in the center of 4 of the patties. Place ½ ounce blue cheese into each indentation, top each with another patty, and gently form into 1¼-inch-thick burgers, making sure to seal all open edges. Cover the burgers with plastic wrap, and refrigerate until needed.

Just before grilling, lightly season the burgers with salt and pepper, then coat with Quick Barbecue Sauce. Grill the burgers over a medium wood or charcoal fire. Cook to the desired doneness: 4 to 5 minutes on each side for rare, 6 to 7 minutes on each side for medium, and 9 to 10 minutes on each side for well-done. Frequently baste the burgers during the grilling with Quick Barbecue Sauce. (This burger may also be cooked on a well-seasoned flat griddle or in a large nonstick sauté pan over medium-high heat. Cook for about the same amount of time as listed for grilling.)

Remove the burgers from the grill, and baste with the remaining Quick Barbecue Sauce. Toast the rolls, cut side down, on the grill or griddle or in a nonstick sauté pan until golden brown, about 1 minute. Place each burger on the bottom half of a toasted roll, and top with Sautéed Mushrooms and the other half of the roll. Serve the burgers immediately with Cheese Fries and frosty mugs of Budweiser.

Quick Barbecue Sauce

Yields 2/3 cup

4 tablespoons ketchup
4 tablespoons light brown sugar
2 tablespoons spicy brown mustard
2 tablespoons dark molasses
2 tablespoons cider vinegar
2 cloves garlic, peeled and crushed

Heat all the ingredients in a 2-quart saucepan over medium-high heat. Bring the mixture to a boil, then adjust the heat and allow to simmer for 30 minutes, stirring frequently. Remove the pan from the heat, then remove and discard the garlic cloves. The sauce may be used immediately or cooled in an ice-water bath. It will keep tightly covered in the refrigerator for several days. Warm the sauce before using.

Sautéed Mushrooms

Yields 4 servings

2 tablespoons unsalted butter
2 tablespoons minced onions
2 tablespoons minced shallots
8 ounces sliced fresh mushrooms
  Salt and pepper to season
2 tablespoons beer

Heat the butter in a medium nonstick sauté pan over medium-high heat. When the butter has melted, add the onions and shallots, and cook until they are tender, about 2 to 3 minutes. Add the mushrooms, season with salt and pepper, and sauté until most of the moisture has evaporated, about 3 to 4 minutes.

Add the beer to the mixture, then add salt and pepper to taste.

The mushrooms may be used immediately or cooled and rewarmed when needed.

Cheese Fries

Yields 4 servings

3 large Idaho potatoes, washed and scrubbed clean
1 cup vegetable oil
  Salt and pepper to season
4 tablespoons beer
8 ounces grated Tillamook cheddar cheese (see Note)
1 teaspoon Tabasco Sauce
4 slices crisp bacon, crumbled

Use a sharp knife to cut the potatoes into 1/4-inch-thick slices. Cut the slices into 1/4-inch-thick strips. The potatoes may be fried immediately or covered with cold water and refrigerated for several hours.

Preheat the oven to 250°F.

Heat the vegetable oil in a large heavy-duty skillet or large sauté pan over high heat to a temperature of 375°F. While the oil is heating, drain and thoroughly dry the potatoes on paper towels.

Fry the potatoes in the hot oil, one-half the amount at a time, until crispy and golden brown, about 6 to 7 minutes. Drain on paper towels, and season with salt and pepper. Hold the potatoes in the preheated oven while preparing the cheese.

Heat 1 inch water in the bottom half of a double boiler over low heat. Heat the beer in the top half of the double boiler. When hot, add the cheddar. Use a rubber spatula to constantly stir the cheese until smooth, about 4 minutes. Add the Tabasco Sauce and stir to combine.

Remove the fries from the oven and place on a serving plate. Pour the cheese over the fries, then garnish with the bacon. Serve immediately.

The fries may be held in the preheated oven for up to 30 minutes. However, the cheese should be prepared just moments before serving the Cheese Fries.

Note: Oregon Tillamook cheddar cheese has no peers. Its firm, smooth texture and medium-sharp flavor make for successful cheddar cheese cookery. Any favorite cheddar cheese can be used in this recipe.

Sicilian Burger

with Semolina Olive Buns and Marinated Cauliflower Salad

Makes 4 burgers

Sanford D'Amato
Chef/Owner
Sanford Restaurant
Milwaukee, Wisconsin

SOME MIGHT SAY THAT SANFORD D'AMATO WALKED IMMEDIATELY INTO THE LIMELIGHT. THE TRUTH IS THAT SANFORD TOILED MANY YEARS IN A VARIETY OF FOOD-SERVICE OPERATIONS, BEGINNING IN HIS TEENS IN MILWAUKEE-AREA RESTAURANTS. AFTER GRADUATING FROM THE CULINARY INSTITUTE OF AMERICA, HE COOKED AND HONED HIS CRAFT IN RESTAURANTS IN NEW YORK CITY BEFORE RETURNING TO MILWAUKEE, WHERE HE DREAMED OF OPENING HIS OWN RESTAURANT. HE ACCOMPLISHED THAT GOAL IN 1989, WHEN HE AND HIS WIFE, ANGELA, OPENED SANFORD RESTAURANT IN A BUILDING THAT AT ONE TIME HOUSED HIS GRANDFATHER'S GROCERY STORE.

SINCE THAT DAY, SANFORD'S RESTAURANT HAS ACHIEVED MUCH NATIONAL RECOGNITION, INCLUDING A LISTING IN *ESQUIRE* MAGAZINE AS ONE OF THE NATION'S BEST NEW RESTAURANTS.

SANFORD'S SICILIAN BURGER WAS INSPIRED BY THE BURGERS HIS GRANDFATHER MADE FOR HIM AT THE GROCERY STORE WHERE HE HAD WORKED AS A YOUNGSTER.

4 tablespoons extra-virgin olive oil
1/2 cup finely minced onions
1/4 cup dry white wine
2 tablespoons sweet Marsala wine
1 small bay leaf
1 teaspoon freshly ground black pepper
1/2 teaspoon salt
1 pound ground beef chuck
1/2 pound ground pork

1 large egg, lightly beaten
1/4 cup dry white bread crumbs
1/4 cup grated imported Romano cheese
2 tablespoons chopped fresh parsley
1 tablespoon chopped fresh basil
Salt and freshly ground black pepper to season

Heat 2 tablespoons olive oil in a small nonstick sauté pan over medium-high heat. When hot, add the onions and cook until translucent, about 3 to 4 minutes. Add the white wine, Marsala wine, bay leaf, 1 teaspoon freshly ground black pepper, and 1/2 teaspoon salt. Bring the mixture to a boil, then adjust the heat and allow to simmer until most of the liquid has evaporated, about 9 to 10 minutes. Discard the bay leaf. Transfer the onion mixture to a dinner plate and place uncovered in the refrigerator to cool.

In a 5-quart stainless steel bowl, gently but thoroughly combine the ground beef, ground pork, chilled onion mixture, egg, bread crumbs, Romano, parsley, and basil.

Gently form the seasoned ground meat mixture into four 7-ounce, 1 1/4-inch-thick burgers. Cover the burgers with plastic wrap and refrigerate until needed.

Just before grilling, lightly season the burgers with salt and freshly ground black pepper. Grill the burgers over a medium wood or charcoal fire. Cook to the desired doneness: 6 to 7 minutes on each side for medium, and 9 to 10 minutes on each side for medium-well. (This burger may also be cooked on a well-seasoned flat griddle or in a large nonstick sauté pan over medium-high heat. Cook for about the same amount of time as listed for grilling.)

Remove the burgers from the grill. Cut 4 Semolina Olive Buns in half. Lightly brush the bun halves with the remaining olive oil. Toast the buns, oil side down, on the grill or griddle or in a nonstick sauté pan until golden, about 1 minute. Serve the Sicilian Burgers on the toasted buns, accompanied by the Marinated Cauliflower Salad.

Semolina Olive Buns

Makes 8 buns

1¹/₂	cups warm water
2	tablespoons plus 1 teaspoon extra-virgin olive oil
1	tablespoon barley malt (see Note)
1	teaspoon granulated sugar
2	tablespoons active dry yeast
3	cups bread flour
1¹/₄	cups semolina flour (see Note)
2	teaspoons salt
¹/₂	cup pitted and chopped oil-cured, ripe black olives

In the bowl of an electric mixer, place the warm water, 1 tablespoon olive oil, barley malt, and sugar, and stir gently to dissolve the sugar. Add the yeast and stir to dissolve. Allow the mixture to stand and foam for 5 minutes.

Place the mixing bowl with the yeast mixture on an electric mixer fitted with a dough hook. Add 2¹/₂ cups bread flour, the semolina flour, and salt, and mix on low speed for 1 minute. Stop the mixer and scrape down the bowl. Continue mixing on medium-low speed until the dough is very smooth and elastic, about 5 to 6 minutes. (If a table-model electric mixer is not available, follow the directions using a hand-held mixer or kneading by hand. The mixing times will increase depending upon which alternative method is used.)

Place the dough on a clean, dry, lightly floured work surface, using the remaining bread flour as necessary. Flatten the dough. Place the olives on top, fold the dough from end to end, and knead the olives into the dough, about 2 to 3 minutes.

Coat the inside of a 5-quart stainless steel bowl with 1 teaspoon olive oil. Place the dough in the bowl and wipe the bowl with the dough. Cover the bowl with plastic wrap. Allow the dough to rise in a warm location until it has doubled in volume, about 1 hour.

Preheat the oven to 325°F.

Place the dough on a lightly floured work surface. Use a sharp knife to cut the dough into 8 equal portions. Shape each portion into a ball. Place the balls on a baking sheet lined with parchment paper. Loosely cover the dough with plastic wrap and allow to rise in a warm location until doubled in size, about 30 minutes.

Using a dough cutter or the back side of a thin-bladed knife, press an X on the top of each bun (be sure not to cut the buns). Allow the buns to rise for an additional 10 minutes. Brush with the remaining tablespoon olive oil.

Bake the buns for 35 to 40 minutes, until golden brown.

Allow the buns to cool thoroughly before cutting in half.

The buns will keep fresh for 2 to 3 days stored in a sealable plastic bag at room temperature.

Note: Look for barley malt and semolina flour in health-food stores, or in the health-food section at your supermarket.

Marinated Cauliflower Salad

Yields 4 servings

2   cups water
1   cup red wine vinegar
1/3 cup granulated sugar
4   cloves garlic, peeled
2   small bay leaves
2   small sprigs fresh thyme
1   small sprig fresh rosemary
3   whole allspice berries, crushed
2   whole cloves
1   tablespoon cracked black pepper
1   teaspoon kosher salt
2   cups small cauliflower florets
1   cup thinly sliced carrots
1/2 cup diced red onions
1/2 cup julienned red bell peppers
1   cup sliced green Sicilian brine-cured olives
1/2 cup seeded and sliced peperoncini (see Note)
2   teaspoons capers, rinsed and chopped
1   cup extra-virgin olive oil
1/2 cup thinly sliced basil leaves
    Salt and freshly ground black pepper
    to season

To prepare the marinade, heat the water, red wine vinegar, sugar, garlic, bay leaves, thyme, rosemary, allspice, cloves, cracked black pepper, and kosher salt in a 4-quart stainless steel or other noncorrosive saucepan over high heat. Bring the mixture to a boil. Remove the pan from the heat, cover, and allow to stand for 30 minutes. Strain (and reserve) the marinade through a fine mesh strainer or several folds of cheesecloth.

Return the marinade to the saucepan. Add the cauliflower, carrots, onions, and red bell peppers, and return the saucepan to high heat. As soon as the mixture boils, remove the pan from the heat. Add the olives, peperoncini, and capers. Allow to cool at room temperature. When cool, cover and refrigerate until thoroughly chilled, about 1 hour. Drain the vegetables through a colander.

In a stainless steel or other noncorrosive bowl, toss the vegetables with the olive oil and basil. Season to taste with salt and freshly ground black pepper, and serve immediately.

This salad will keep tightly covered in the refrigerator for several days.

Note: Peperoncini are small hot and sweet peppers sold in their pickling juice. They are available in Italian groceries or gourmet food markets.

> *Food-related childhood memories abound for Sanford. A common sight in his family's grocery store was the large glass jars containing a colorful mix of pickled vegetables known as giardiniera. If only Grandfather could taste this salad!*

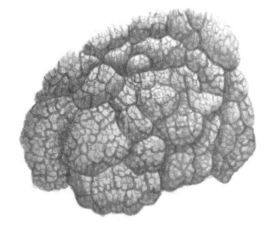

51

///////////////// Shiitake Mushroom Burger \\\\\\\\\\\\\\\\\

with Black-Eyed Pea and Roasted Pepper Salad and
Crispy Potato Cakes

Makes 8 burgers

Marcel Desaulniers
Chef/Co-Owner
The Trellis Restaurant
Williamsburg, Virginia

AFTER MARCEL DESAULNIERS GRADUATED AT THE AGE OF NINETEEN FROM THE CULINARY INSTITUTE, HE CAME TO THE BIG APPLE TO HONE HIS CRAFT. FOLLOWING A YEAR OF COOKING AT PRIVATE CLUBS IN NEW YORK, HE WAS ASKED TO HONE A CRAFT OF A DIFFERENT KIND WHEN HE WAS DRAFTED INTO THE U.S. MARINE CORPS. FOLLOWING A TOUR OF DUTY IN VIETNAM, WHERE HIS ONLY MEALS WERE C RATIONS, MARCEL RETURNED TO NEW YORK CITY TO WORK AT THE PIERRE HOTEL. IN 1970, HE WENT TO VIRGINIA TO WORK FOR THE COLONIAL WILLIAMSBURG FOUNDATION'S RESTAURANT OPERATIONS.

IN WILLIAMSBURG, MARCEL OBSERVED, RELISHED, AND INSPIRED THE REBIRTH OF AMERICAN CUISINE. HE OPENED THE TRELLIS RESTAURANT IN 1980 AND HAS RECEIVED ACCOLADES EVER SINCE.

SOME SAY MARCEL IS A CULINARY PARADOX, HAVING AUTHORED THE WILDLY POPULAR *DEATH BY CHOCOLATE* WHILE PRACTICING A NEARLY MONASTICAL REGIME OF HEALTHY EATING. HIS THEORY IS THAT FOOD CAN BE BOTH HEALTHY AND DELICIOUS...BUT AN OCCASIONAL INDULGENCE IS GOOD FOR THE SOUL.

HIS BURGER IS AN EXAMPLE OF HEALTHY EATING THAT HAS ALL THE QUALITIES OF SERIOUS INDULGENCE.

1 cup dried black-eyed peas, washed and picked over
1 large Idaho potato
3 tablespoons extra-virgin olive oil
2 shallots, minced

2 pounds fresh shiitake mushrooms, stemmed and sliced thin (see Note)
Salt and pepper to season
2 tablespoons chopped fresh parsley
2 teaspoons chopped fresh thyme

Soak the black-eyed peas overnight in 1 quart cold water.

Rinse and drain the soaked peas. Place in a 2-quart saucepan and cover with 1 quart lightly salted water. Bring to a boil over high heat, adjust the heat, and allow the peas to simmer until very tender, about 35 minutes. Drain the peas. Transfer to a dinner plate and place uncovered in the refrigerator to cool.

In a 2-quart saucepan, cover the potato with 1 quart cold water. Bring to a boil over high heat, adjust the heat, and allow the potato to simmer until cooked through, about 35 to 40 minutes. Transfer to a dinner plate and place uncovered in the refrigerator to cool, about 1 hour.

Heat 2 tablespoons olive oil in a large nonstick sauté pan over medium heat. When hot, add the shallots and sauté for 1 minute. Add the shiitake mushrooms, then season with salt and pepper. Adjust the heat to medium-high and sauté until very tender, about 7 to 8 minutes. Transfer to a dinner plate and place uncovered in the refrigerator to cool.

Peel and grate the thoroughly cooled potato. Combine 8 ounces grated potato (the whole peeled potato may yield slightly more; use only the specified 8 ounces) with the cooked black-eyed peas, sautéed shiitake mushrooms, parsley, and thyme in a 5-quart stainless steel bowl. Season with salt and pepper. Mix well using your hands (be certain to thoroughly combine the ingredients, squashing some of the peas while mixing).

Gently form the mushroom mixture into eight 6-ounce, 1¼-inch-thick burgers. Cover the burgers with plastic wrap and refrigerate until needed.

Preheat the oven to 350°F.

Heat a large nonstick sauté pan that has been lightly brushed with the remaining 1 tablespoon olive oil over medium-high heat. Sear 4 of the burgers in the hot pan until crispy and golden brown, about 2 minutes on each side. Transfer the burgers to a baking sheet. Repeat the procedure with the remaining 4 burgers, then place on the baking sheet with the other burgers and bake until heated through, about 12 to 14 minutes.

Portion Black-Eyed Pea and Roasted Pepper Salad onto 8 dinner plates. Place Crispy Potato Cakes in the centers of the salads, then set the burgers on the potato cakes. Serve immediately.

Note: Until just a few years ago, shiitake mushrooms were marketed primarily in the dried form. Today, one can find fresh shiitake mushrooms in almost any good supermarket's produce department. A cooked shiitake tastes at once silky and smooth, and as it is chewed, it has a nutty, almost meatlike impression.

Shiitake mushrooms are available virtually year-round. They can be stored in the refrigerator for 2 to 4 weeks, depending upon the moisture content when they are harvested. They will, however, lose some of their woodsy aroma the longer they are stored.

> *Shiitake mushrooms are wonderful conveyors of flavor. In this recipe, the essence of the shallots and the herbal tones of the parsley and thyme form a subtle confluence with the mushrooms and black-eyed peas. The result is so divine that it could convert one to a vegetarian diet.*

> *A glass of California Sauvignon Blanc would be the perfect complement to each wonderful Shiitake Mushroom Burger.*

> *Black-eyed peas are emblematic of the South. Another legume also associated with the southern region is peanuts. In keeping with the spirit, you may want to sprinkle a few toasted Virginia peanuts over this salad.*

Black-Eyed Pea and Roasted Pepper Salad

Yields 8 servings

¼	cup dried black-eyed peas, washed and picked over (see Note)
1	cup extra-virgin olive oil
¼	cup balsamic vinegar
2	tablespoons whole-grain mustard
1	teaspoon salt
1	teaspoon cracked black pepper
2	large red bell peppers, roasted, skinned, seeded, and cut into ¼-inch pieces
2	heads curly endive, cut into 2-inch pieces, washed, and dried

Soak the black-eyed peas overnight in 1 quart cold water.

Drain and rinse the soaked peas. Place in a 2-quart saucepan, and cover with 1 quart lightly salted water. Bring to a boil over high heat. Adjust the heat and simmer the peas until very tender, about 35 minutes. Drain the peas, transfer to a dinner plate, and place uncovered in the refrigerator to cool.

In a 5-quart stainless steel bowl, whisk together the olive oil, balsamic vinegar, mustard, salt, and pepper. Add the cooled black-eyed peas and red bell pepper pieces. Use a rubber spatula to combine thoroughly. Add the curly endive pieces and toss to coat the greens. Serve immediately. The salad may be stored tightly covered in the refrigerator for several hours.

Note: Although I call for dried black-eyed peas in this recipe, you may certainly substitute fresh peas when available (primarily during the summer months). If you are using fresh peas, skip the soaking step and boil them until tender.

Crispy Potato Cakes

Makes 8 cakes

4 **large Idaho potatoes**
1 **large egg, lightly beaten**
   Salt and pepper to season
2 **tablespoons olive oil**

In a 2-quart saucepan, cover 1 of the potatoes with 1 quart cold water, and bring to a boil over high heat. Adjust the heat, and simmer the potato until cooked through, about 35 to 40 minutes. Transfer to a dinner plate and place uncovered in the refrigerator to cool, about 1 hour.

Peel and grate the thoroughly cooled potato into a 5-quart stainless steel bowl. Add 2 tablespoons beaten egg (an average large egg will yield about 4 tablespoons), season with salt and pepper, and stir well to combine. Store in the refrigerator until needed.

In a 6-quart saucepan, heat 4 quarts lightly salted water to a boil.

While the water is heating, thoroughly wash the remaining 3 potatoes (do not peel). Trim the ends of the potatoes so that they are flat. Cut the potatoes, one at a time, into long, thin strands on a Japanese turning slicer fitted with a medium-tooth blade. Immediately place the potato strands in cold water.

Drain the potato strands in a colander. Lightly blanch the potatoes by placing them into the boiling water for 60 seconds. Drain the blanched potatoes and place them on a baking sheet that has been lined with paper towels. Place uncovered in the refrigerator to cool. When thoroughly cool, remove any excess moisture from the potatoes by patting them dry with paper towels.

Gently but thoroughly combine the potato egg mixture with the blanched potato strands. Form the potatoes into eight 3-ounce, ½-inch-thick cakes. The cakes may be cooked immediately or covered with plastic wrap and stored in the refrigerator for up to 24 hours.

Preheat the oven to 200°F.

Heat a large nonstick sauté pan that has been lightly brushed with the olive oil over high heat. Season the cakes with salt and pepper. When the pan is hot, pan-fry the cakes, 4 at a time, until golden brown and crispy, about 9 to 10 minutes on each side. Keep the cakes warm in the oven while repeating the cooking procedure with the remaining 4 cakes (or if you have 2 large nonstick sauté pans, do all 8 cakes simultaneously). Serve immediately.

The cakes may be held warm in the oven for up to 45 minutes after being pan-fried.

Low-Country Rabbit Burger
with Carrot Wheat Bread, Pecan Butter, and Celery
and Belgian Endive Salad

Makes 4 burgers

Robert Dickson
Chef/Owner
Robert's of Charleston
Charleston, South Carolina

ROBERT DICKSON IS AN IMPRESARIO OF DISTINCTIVE MAGNITUDE. CHEF/OWNER OF HIS INTERNATIONALLY ACCLAIMED EPONYMOUS RESTAURANT, ROBERT IS AT CENTER STAGE EVERY EVENING, ENJOYING HIS ROLE AS CHEF, RESTAURATEUR, AND ACCOMPLISHED OPERA SINGER.

FOLLOWING HIS GRADUATION FROM THE INSTITUTE IN 1963, ROBERT COOKED FOR AND WITH SOME OF THE NOTABLES OF THE FOOD WORLD, NOT THE LEAST BEING JULIA CHILD. HOWEVER, ROBERT'S LOVE AND TALENT FOR OPERA LED HIM TO LONDON, WHERE HE STUDIED OPERA FOR SEVERAL YEARS. NOT WISHING TO EXPATRIATE, ROBERT RETURNED STATESIDE IN 1976 TO COMBINE HIS TWO LOVES AT ROBERT'S OF CHARLESTON. THE REST, AS THEY SAY, IS HISTORY.

THE ALMOST MELODIC INTONATIONS OF ROBERT'S LOW-COUNTRY RABBIT BURGER AND ITS ACCOMPANIMENTS ARE INDICATIVE OF THIS GENTLE MAN'S NATURE.

Rhône wines are all the rage these days. Robert suggests an exuberantly fruity and light red Côtes du Rhône of recent vintage.

½	**cup Carrot Wheat Bread bread crumbs**
¼	**cup cold chicken stock**
1	**pound boned and trimmed rabbit meat from loin sections, cut into 1-inch pieces (or 1 pound ground rabbit meat; see Note)**
2	**ounces salt-cured ham, finely chopped**
½	**cup minced onions**
2	**tablespoons minced shallots**
1	**teaspoon chopped fresh thyme**
½	**teaspoon cracked black pepper**
½	**teaspoon celery salt Salt and freshly ground black pepper to season**

In a small stainless steel bowl, combine the bread crumbs and cold chicken stock. Cover with plastic wrap and refrigerate.

If using rabbit pieces, grind through a meat grinder fitted with a coarse grinding plate into a 5-quart stainless steel bowl.

Gently but thoroughly combine the ground rabbit with the ham, chilled bread crumb mixture, onions, shallots, thyme, cracked black pepper, and celery salt.

Gently form the seasoned rabbit into four 6-ounce, 1-inch-thick burgers. Cover the burgers with plastic wrap and refrigerate until needed.

Preheat the oven to 350°F.

Just before cooking the burgers, lightly season them with salt and freshly ground black pepper. Heat a large nonstick sauté pan over medium-high heat. When hot, pan-sear the burgers until golden brown, about 5 to 6 minutes on each side. Transfer the rabbit burgers to a baking sheet and finish cooking in the oven, about 4 to 5 minutes. Toast 8 slices of Carrot Wheat Bread. This may be done in a toaster or in the oven with the burgers for about 3 to 4 minutes. Spread the toasted slices with Pecan Butter. Serve each burger in between

2 slices of toasted and buttered Carrot Wheat Bread, accompanied by Celery and Belgian Endive Salad.

Note: A medium-size eviscerated rabbit will weigh between 2½ and 3 pounds. The yield of trimmed meat from such a rabbit will be 10 to 14 ounces, which means you will need at least 2 rabbits to complete this recipe. Use the leftover rabbit for a stew or as part of a mixed grill.

Carrot Wheat Bread

Makes 2 loaves (thirty-two ½-inch slices)

²⁄₃ **cup milk**
3 **tablespoons unsalted butter, melted, plus 4 teaspoons unsalted butter, softened**
2 **tablespoons granulated sugar**
2 **teaspoons salt**
5 **teaspoons active dry yeast**
1 **cup warm water**
2 **cups finely grated raw peeled carrots**
¼ **cup chopped toasted pecans**
1 **large egg, lightly beaten**
2 **cups whole wheat flour**
4½ **cups bread flour**

Heat the milk in a small saucepan over medium-high heat. Bring to a simmer. Remove from heat and add 3 tablespoons melted butter, sugar, and salt. Stir to dissolve the sugar. Transfer to a small bowl and allow to cool to room temperature.

In a 5-quart stainless steel bowl, dissolve the yeast in the warm water. Allow to stand and foam for 6 to 7 minutes. Add the milk mixture to the yeast. Use a rubber spatula to stir in the carrots, pecans, and egg. Add the whole wheat flour and 1 cup bread flour. Stir until smooth. Add an additional 3 cups bread flour and combine by hand until the mixture becomes a soft dough.

Knead the dough until smooth and elastic, about 6 to 8 minutes, on a clean, dry, lightly floured work surface, using the remaining ½ cup bread flour as necessary. Coat the inside of a 5-quart stainless steel bowl with 2 tea-spoons softened butter. Place the dough into the bowl and wipe the bowl with the dough. Cover the bowl with plastic wrap and place it in a warm location. Allow the dough to rise until it has doubled in size, about 1 hour.

On a clean, dry work surface that has been dusted with bread flour, punch the dough down to its original size and divide into 2 equal portions. Form each portion into a loaf, and place each loaf into a 9- by 5- by 3-inch loaf pan that has been coated with 1 teaspoon softened butter. Cover each pan with plastic wrap. Allow the dough to rise in a warm location until it reaches the top of the loaf pans, about 45 minutes.

Preheat the oven to 375°F.

Bake the bread on the middle rack of the oven until golden brown, about 30 to 35 minutes. Cool the loaves in the loaf pans for 15 minutes before removing. When removed, allow to cool to room temperature on wire racks before slicing.

To test bread for doneness, lightly tap the bottom of the loaf; a hollow sound indicates that the bread is done.

One loaf of this bread will provide both the bread crumbs for the ground rabbit mixture and the sliced bread on which to serve the burgers. However, Robert believes in taking advantage of a good thing, so his recipe yields 2 loaves. You can freeze the extra loaf or serve it warm on a Sunday morning with Pecan Butter or orange marmalade.

Pecan Butter

Yields 1 cup

1 teaspoon salt
¹/₂ cup shredded carrots
¹/₄ cup chopped toasted pecans
4 ounces unsalted butter, softened

Heat 3 cups water and the salt to a boil in a 2-quart saucepan over high heat. Cook the carrots in the boiling water until tender, about 1 minute. Drain the carrots, then transfer to a dinner plate and place uncovered in the refrigerator to cool.

In a stainless steel bowl, combine the cooled carrots with the pecans and butter. Stir with a rubber spatula until well blended. The butter can be stored covered in the refrigerator for up to 2 weeks.

Celery and Belgian Endive Salad

Yields 4 servings

3 tablespoons sherry wine vinegar
¹/₂ teaspoon celery seeds
¹/₂ teaspoon chopped fresh thyme
¹/₂ teaspoon salt
¹/₄ teaspoon white pepper
¹/₂ cup peanut oil
2 heads Belgian endive, cored and sliced thin diagonally
3 stalks celery, sliced thin diagonally
1 small red onion, sliced thin

In a stainless steel bowl, whisk together the sherry wine vinegar, celery seeds, thyme, salt, and pepper. Continue to whisk the mixture while pouring in a slow, steady stream of the peanut oil. Add the Belgian endive, celery, and red onions. Toss with the dressing to coat lightly, and serve immediately.

> Belgian endive oxidizes and discolors quickly. For this reason, the salad should be prepared just prior to cooking the burgers. If you need a bit more time, prepare the salad as directed, but cut and add the endive to the salad at the last moment. The prepared salad without the endive will keep covered in the refrigerator for several hours before serving.

Peacock Alley Tuna Burger
with Sesame Brioche and Sesame Ginger Dressing

Makes 4 burgers

John Doherty
Executive Chef
The Waldorf-Astoria
New York, New York

AS THE YOUNGEST AND ONLY AMERICAN-BORN EXECUTIVE CHEF TO OVERSEE THE KITCHENS OF THE WALDORF-ASTORIA, JOHN DOHERTY IS ACCUSTOMED TO TURNING HEADS. A MODEL OF PROFESSIONALISM AND BONHOMIE, JOHN HAS ALSO BEEN A MODEL OF OTHER SORTS, FEATURED IN *M* MAGAZINE ATTIRED BOTH IN TRADITIONAL CHEF'S GARB AND IN A BUSINESS SUIT IN A PICTORIAL OF CURRENT MEN'S FASHIONS. MOST OF THE TIME, HOWEVER, JOHN CAN BE FOUND SUPERVISING THE WALDORF KITCHENS, WHICH PRODUCE THOUSANDS OF MEALS A DAY FOR SOME OF THE MOST PROMINENT PEOPLE IN THE WORLD.

> *A garnish of delicate Bibb lettuce leaves is particularly compatible with this burger.*

> *These tuna burgers also make wonderful hors d'oeuvres. Serve pan-seared, tiny ½-ounce tuna burgers with a black-olive paste (check your favorite tapenade recipe) on grilled Focaccia (see page 82). Garnish with arugula.*

1¼ pounds fresh tuna fillet, cut into 1-inch pieces (or 1¼ pounds ground tuna fillet)

5 tablespoons chopped fresh chives

3 tablespoons finely chopped shallots

1 tablespoon extra-virgin olive oil

1 tablespoon soy sauce

1 tablespoon dry red wine

1 teaspoon grated fresh horseradish root

3 dashes Worcestershire sauce
Salt and pepper to season

If using tuna pieces, grind through a meat grinder fitted with a coarse grinding plate into a 5-quart stainless steel bowl.

Gently but thoroughly combine the ground tuna with the chives, shallots, olive oil, soy sauce, red wine, horseradish, Worcestershire sauce, and salt and pepper to season.

Gently form the seasoned ground tuna into four 5½- to 6-ounce, 1-inch-thick burgers. Cover the burgers with plastic wrap and refrigerate until needed.

Heat a well-seasoned flat griddle or a large nonstick sauté pan over medium-high heat. When hot, cook the burgers for 1½ to 2 minutes on each side for rare, 2½ to 3 minutes on each side for medium-rare, and about 4 minutes on each side for medium. Toast 8 slices of Sesame Brioche on the griddle or in a nonstick sauté pan until golden brown, about 1 minute.

Serve the tuna burgers on the toasted Sesame Brioche with a ramekin of Sesame Ginger Dressing on the side.

Sesame Brioche

Makes 1 loaf (16 ½-inch slices)

4   **cups all-purpose flour**
2   **teaspoons salt**
2   **tablespoons plus 1 teaspoon toasted sesame seeds**
2   **tablespoons granulated sugar**
½   **cup warm water**
2   **tablespoons active dry yeast**
4   **large eggs**
12   **tablespoons plus 1 teaspoon unsalted butter, softened**
1   **tablespoon cold water**

Sift the flour onto wax paper. Remeasure 4 cups sifted flour (there will be more sifted flour than the necessary 4 cups; reserve the remainder for later use). Sift the remeasured 4 cups together with the salt. Add 2 tablespoons sesame seeds to the sifted flour and set aside.

In the bowl of an electric mixer, dissolve the sugar in the warm water. Add the yeast and stir gently to dissolve. Allow the mixture to stand and foam for 2 to 3 minutes.

Place the mixing bowl on an electric mixer fitted with a dough hook. On top of the yeast mixture, add the sifted flour mixture and 3 eggs. Combine on low speed for 1 minute. Scrape down the sides of the bowl, then continue to mix on low speed until dough forms a ball, about 2 minutes. Adjust the mixer speed to medium, and begin to add 12 tablespoons butter, one tablespoon at a time, being certain each tablespoon is thoroughly incorporated before adding the next (for more efficient incorporation of the butter, periodically stop the mixer and pull the dough off the hook). Continue to add the butter until all 12 tablespoons have been incorporated into the dough, 12 to 14 minutes.

Remove the bowl from the mixer and also remove the dough hook from the dough. Cover the mixing bowl with a towel and place in a warm location. Allow the dough to rise until it has doubled in volume, about 1 hour. Punch down the dough to its original size, transfer to a pie tin lined with plastic wrap, cover the dough with plastic wrap, and place in the freezer for 15 minutes.

Preheat the oven to 325°F.

Flour a clean, dry work surface with some of the reserved sifted flour. Place the dough on the work surface and divide it into 3 equal pieces. Using your hands, roll each piece into a long ropelike strand about 14 to 15 inches long and 1½ inches thick. Braid the 3 pieces of dough together. Coat a loaf pan with the remaining teaspoon butter. Put the braided dough into the loaf pan and place in a warm location. Allow the dough to rise until it has doubled in volume, about 30 minutes. Whisk the remaining egg with 1 tablespoon cold water, then gently and lightly brush the top of the dough with this egg wash. Sprinkle the remaining teaspoon sesame seeds over the top of the dough.

Bake the brioche loaf in the center of the oven for 30 minutes. Allow the baked loaf to cool in the pan for 15 minutes before removing from pan. Remove the brioche from the loaf pan and allow to cool to room temperature before slicing.

To test the brioche for doneness, gently remove the loaf from the baking pan. Lightly tap the bottom of the loaf; a hollow sound will indicate that the bread is done.

> *An electric mixer fitted with a dough hook is an essential piece of equipment for the successful preparation of high-quality brioche, a yeast-raised bread enriched with eggs. If such a mixer is not in residence in your equipment cupboard, consider an alternative bread such as traditional challah.*

Sesame Ginger Dressing

Yields I cup

¹/₄ **cup water**
 1 **teaspoon granulated sugar**
 1 **teaspoon finely minced fresh ginger**
³/₄ **cup mayonnaise**
 1 **tablespoon sesame oil (see Note)**
  Salt and pepper to season

Heat the water and sugar in a 2¹/₂-quart saucepan over medium heat. Bring to a boil. Add the ginger and allow to cook until the ginger is tender, about 1 minute. Remove the mixture from the heat and cool in an ice-water bath.

In a stainless steel bowl, whisk together the mayonnaise and cold ginger-water mixture. Slowly whisk the sesame oil into the ginger-mayonnaise mixture. Adjust the seasoning with salt and pepper, and combine thoroughly. Cover with plastic wrap and refrigerate for at least 6 hours before using.

Note: Look for sesame oil in Asian grocery stores. Purchase oil that is packaged in glass bottles or cans rather than plastic bottles (the oil has a tendency to turn rancid more quickly in plastic packaging).

> *John Doherty's Sesame Ginger Dressing adds a piquant and delicious touch to a favorite selection of the luncheon crowd at The Waldorf-Astoria's Peacock Alley.*

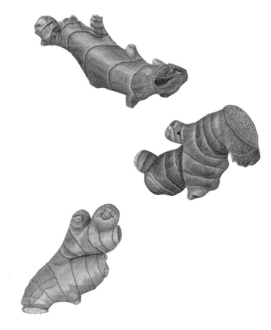

Southern Fried Chicken Burger

with Honey Mustard Mayonnaise and Toasted Peanut and Sweet Corn Salad

Makes 4 burgers

Mark Erickson
Executive Chef
Cherokee Town and Country Club
Atlanta, Georgia

AFTER WORKING AS SOUS CHEF AT THE GREENBRIER RESORT IN WHITE SULPHUR SPRINGS, WEST VIRGINIA, IN THE EARLY 1980S, MARK RETURNED TO THE CULINARY INSTITUTE OF AMERICA TO TEACH. A CERTIFIED MASTER CHEF, HE WAS ALSO THE OPENING CHEF FOR THE INSTITUTE'S NUTRITIONAL RESTAURANT, THE SAINT ANDREW'S CAFE. IN 1990, MARK BECAME THE EXECUTIVE CHEF OF THE CHEROKEE TOWN AND COUNTRY CLUB IN ATLANTA, WHERE HE IS PUTTING A NEW TWIST TO REGIONAL CUISINE. WITH THIS RECIPE, HE OFFERS GUESTS OF THE VENERABLE CLUB SOME REAL "SOUTHERN COMFORT."

If you are not in the mood for a ground chicken burger, then Mark suggests using a whole 4-ounce boneless and skinless chicken breast. You may either pan-sear or grill the breast. But of course, frying it as suggested for the chicken burger will also result in good eating.

1¼ **pounds boneless and skinless chicken breast meat, trimmed of fat and cut into 1-inch pieces (or 1¼ pounds ground chicken breast meat)**
1 **medium egg white**
3 **tablespoons buttermilk**
1 **small clove garlic, minced**
1 **teaspoon salt**

1 **teaspoon freshly ground black pepper**
1½ **cups dry bread crumbs**
1 **cup peanut oil**
4 **Best Burger Buns (see page 109), cut in half, or 8 slices cornbread**
8 **iceberg lettuce leaves, washed and dried**
4 **¼-inch-thick slices ripe tomatoes**

If using chicken pieces, grind through a meat grinder fitted with a coarse grinding plate into a 5-quart stainless steel bowl.

In a separate bowl, whisk together the egg white, buttermilk, garlic, salt, and pepper. Add this mixture and ½ cup bread crumbs to the ground chicken meat. Combine the ingredients gently but thoroughly.

Gently form the chicken mixture into four 5-ounce, 1-inch-thick burgers. Cover the burgers with plastic wrap and refrigerate until needed.

Preheat the oven to 300°F.

Heat the peanut oil in a large nonstick sauté pan over medium-high heat. Lightly coat the chicken burgers with the remaining 1 cup bread crumbs. When the oil is hot, cook 2 of the burgers at a time for 1 minute on each side. Place the chicken burgers on a baking sheet in the oven for 12 to 14 minutes.

Toast the buns, cut side down, in a nonstick sauté pan over medium-high heat until golden brown, about 1 minute.

Spread each top and bottom bun half with Honey Mustard Mayonnaise. Place a chicken burger on the bottom half of each bun. Top each burger with 2 of the lettuce leaves and a slice of the tomato. Top with the other half of the bun and serve with Toasted Peanut and Sweet Corn Salad.

Honey Mustard Mayonnaise

Yields 1 1/3 cups

3/4 **cup mayonnaise**
6   **tablespoons spicy brown mustard**
3   **tablespoons honey**
    Salt and pepper to season

In a stainless steel bowl, whisk together the mayonnaise, mustard, and honey. Adjust the seasoning with salt and pepper, and combine thoroughly. Cover with plastic wrap and refrigerate until needed.

This easily prepared condiment is also good with other foods. Try it as an accompaniment to a full-flavored fish such as wahoo or as a spread on your favorite sandwich (it is quite good with smoked turkey).

Toasted Peanut and Sweet Corn Salad

Yields 3 1/2 cups

1   **cup unsalted shelled peanuts**
3   **medium ears fresh yellow corn, husk and silk removed**
6   **tablespoons peanut oil**
2   **tablespoons cider vinegar**
1   **small red onion, finely minced**
1   **tablespoon chopped fresh parsley**
    Salt and pepper to season

Preheat the oven to 300°F.

Toast the peanuts on a baking sheet in the oven until golden brown, about 20 to 25 minutes. Keep at room temperature until needed.

Blanch the corn for 2 to 3 minutes in 3 quarts of boiling salted water. Drain and cool under cold running water. When the corn is cool enough to handle, cut away the kernels.

In a stainless steel bowl, whisk together the peanut oil and cider vinegar. Add the toasted peanuts, corn kernels, red onions, and parsley. Adjust the seasoning with salt and pepper, and combine thoroughly. Cover with plastic wrap and refrigerate for several hours before using.

This salad would also be terrific as a side dish with pork chops. Conjure up visions of peanut oil–basted pork chops, slowly cooking over the embers of a hickory wood fire, and you might just find yourself in Mark Erickson's neighborhood.

Mansion Roadhouse Burger
with Dean's Favorite French Fries

Makes 4 burgers

Dean Fearing
Chef
The Mansion on Turtle Creek
Dallas, Texas

DEAN FEARING CONSISTENTLY DAZZLES THE PALATES OF DINERS AT THE INTERNATIONALLY KNOWN MANSION ON TURTLE CREEK IN DALLAS, WHERE HE HAS BEEN EXECUTIVE CHEF SINCE 1987. DEAN'S TRADEMARK IS NEW SOUTHWEST CUISINE, WHICH HE PIONEERED IN DALLAS IN THE EARLY 1980S. DEAN SHARES HIS IMAGINATIVE CUISINE IN TWO COOKBOOKS: *THE MANSION ON TURTLE CREEK COOKBOOK* AND *THE DEAN FEARING'S SOUTHWEST CUISINE*.

THE MANSION ROADHOUSE BURGER RECIPE IS DEAN'S SALUTE TO THE ROADHOUSE CAFÉS AND TRUCK STOPS IN TEXAS WHERE THE DOUBLE CHEESEBURGER BECAME FAMOUS.

> *Dean does allow that his Mansion Roadhouse Burger is a substantial handful, even for Texans. He suggests that you not wear your favorite silk blouse or shirt for this gustatory adventure.*

---

2 **pounds lean ground beef chuck**
Salt and pepper to season
4 **Best Burger Buns (see page 109), cut in half**
2 **tablespoons unsalted butter, melted**
8 **slices American cheese**
2 **tablespoons mayonnaise**
2 **tablespoons yellow mustard**
8 **iceberg lettuce leaves, washed and dried**
4 **¼-inch-thick slices ripe tomatoes**
4 **¼-inch-thick slices yellow onions**
16 **hamburger dill pickle chips**

Gently form the ground beef into eight 4-ounce, ½-inch-thick burgers. Season each burger with salt and pepper. Cover the burgers with plastic wrap and refrigerate until needed.

Preheat the oven to 375°F.

Brush each bun half with the butter. Place the buns, buttered side up, on a baking sheet, and bake until golden brown, about 4 to 5 minutes. Reduce the oven heat to keep the buns warm until needed.

Heat a well-seasoned flat griddle or a large nonstick sauté pan over medium-high heat. When hot, cook the burgers for 3 minutes on one side. Turn the burgers over and place 1 slice of the American cheese on each burger. (This cooking time will yield a medium-rare burger. For rare, cook 2 minutes before turning; for medium, cook about 3½ minutes before turning.) While the cheese is melting, remove the buns from the oven and spread each top bun with mayonnaise and each bottom bun with mustard. When the cheese has melted, place 2 of the burgers, one on top of the other, on the bottom half of each bun. Top each stack of burgers with 2 of the lettuce leaves, 1 slice each of tomato and onion, and 4 of the dill pickle chips. Top with the other half of the bun, and serve with Dean's Favorite French Fries and a bottle of Heinz ketchup.

65

Dean's Favorite French Fries

Yields 4 servings

6   **large Idaho potatoes, washed and scrubbed clean**
8   **cups vegetable oil**
2   **cups all-purpose flour**
2   **teaspoons cayenne pepper**
2   **teaspoons chopped fresh thyme**
1/2 **teaspoon chopped fresh sage**
1/2 **teaspoon salt**
1/4 **teaspoon ground white pepper**
1   **cup milk**
     Salt and pepper to season

Preheat the oven to 425°F.

Use a skewer to pierce the skin of each potato several times (this will prevent the skin from cracking during baking). Place the potatoes on the center rack of the oven, and bake them until soft to the touch when gently squeezed, about 1 hour 15 minutes. Remove the potatoes from the oven and allow them to cool to room temperature. When the potatoes are cool, use a sharp knife to cut each one into sixths lengthwise. Cover with plastic wrap and refrigerate until needed. (The cooled and cut potatoes may be kept refrigerated for a couple of days before using.)

Heat the vegetable oil in a deep fryer (or high-sided, heavy-duty pot) fitted with a deep-frying basket over high heat to a temperature of 360°F.

Thoroughly combine the flour with cayenne pepper, thyme, sage, 1/2 teaspoon salt, and ground white pepper.

Dip the potatoes into the milk and then into the seasoned flour mixture; coat evenly, lightly, and thoroughly. Fry the potatoes in the hot oil, one-fourth the amount at a time, until potatoes are golden brown and crisp, about 1 to 1 1/2 minutes. Drain potatoes on paper towels. Lightly season with salt and pepper, and serve immediately.

The fried potatoes may be held warm in a 250°F oven for 15 to 20 minutes before serving.

> *This recipe is proportioned for spud lovers. If your appetite is not Texan in nature, use 4 Idaho spuds rather than 6.*

New England Maple Barbecued Pork Burger
with Anadama Rolls and Celeriac Chips

Makes 8 burgers

Phyllis Flaherty-Bologna

*Executive Chef for National Accounts
Development
General Foods Foodservice
White Plains, New York*

SEVERAL YEARS AFTER GRADUATION, PHYLLIS FLAHERTY-BOLOGNA RETURNED TO THE CULINARY INSTITUTE OF AMERICA AND SERVED ON ITS FACULTY FOR FIVE YEARS. IN 1987, SHE TOOK THE EXTREMELY CHALLENGING POSITION AS EXECUTIVE CHEF FOR GENERAL FOODS USA.

PLAYING ON THE OLD ADAGE THAT "THE PROOF IS IN THE PUDDING," PHYLLIS BELIEVES THAT THE "PROOF OF THE BURGER IS IN THE BUN." HER ANADAMA ROLLS—HOME BASE FOR HER NEW ENGLAND MAPLE BARBECUED PORK BURGER—CONFIRM HER THEORY.

2½   pounds trimmed fresh pork butt, cut into 1-inch pieces (or 2½ pounds ground trimmed pork butt)

2   teaspoons dry mustard

½   teaspoon dried red pepper flakes
   Salt and white pepper to season

½   cup barbecue sauce (use your favorite sauce or see page 46 for Quick Barbecue Sauce)

½   cup maple syrup

1   tablespoon cider vinegar

1   tablespoon brown sugar

1   teaspoon lemon juice

¼   teaspoon lemon zest

2   tablespoons unsalted butter, melted

If using pork pieces, grind through a meat grinder fitted with a coarse grinding plate into a 5-quart stainless steel bowl.

Gently but thoroughly combine the ground pork with the dry mustard, red pepper flakes, and salt and pepper to season.

Gently form the seasoned pork into eight 5-ounce, 1-inch-thick burgers. Cover the burgers with plastic wrap and refrigerate until needed.

Prepare the maple glaze. Heat the barbecue sauce, maple syrup, cider vinegar, brown sugar, lemon juice, and lemon zest in a 4-quart saucepan over medium-high heat. Bring the mixture to a boil, then adjust the heat and allow to simmer until slightly thickened, about 10 minutes.

Preheat the oven to 325°F.

Heat a well-seasoned flat griddle or a large nonstick sauté pan over medium-high heat. When hot, sear the burgers until well browned, about 2 minutes on each side. Remove the burgers to a large ovenproof pan and baste with one-half the amount of maple glaze. Place the pan in the oven and allow to cook for 20 to 22 minutes.

Cut 8 Anadama Rolls in half. Brush each roll half with melted butter. Toast the rolls, buttered side down, on the griddle or in a nonstick sauté pan over medium-high heat until golden brown, about 1 minute.

Remove the burgers from the oven. Place a pork burger on the bottom half of each roll. Baste the burgers with the remaining maple glaze. Top with the other half of the roll, and serve with the addictive and delectable Celeriac Chips.

Anadama Rolls

Makes 12 rolls

6   cups all-purpose flour
1   cup plus 12 teaspoons yellow cornmeal
1   tablespoon active dry yeast
2½ teaspoons salt
4   tablespoons unsalted butter
2   cups plus 1 tablespoon water
⅓   cup molasses
1   large egg yolk

Combine 5½ cups flour, 1 cup cornmeal, yeast, and salt in the bowl of an electric mixer fitted with a paddle.

With the mixer on low speed, add the butter, 1 tablespoon at a time, and combine the ingredients until the mixture resembles fine crumbs, about 3 minutes. Remove the paddle from the mixer and replace with a dough hook. (If a table-model electric mixer is not available, follow the directions using a hand-held mixer or kneading by hand. The mixing times will increase depending upon which alternative method is used.)

Combine 2 cups hot tap water (about 130°F) and the molasses in a 4-cup measure. Stir with a whisk to dissolve the molasses. Add the molasses mixture to the dry ingredients. Mix on low speed for 5 minutes, stopping the mixer at 1-minute intervals and thoroughly scraping down the sides of the bowl. Mix for an additional 2 to 3 minutes on medium-low speed, until the dough is smooth and no longer sticky.

Remove the bowl from the mixer and cover with a towel or plastic wrap. Allow the dough to rise in a warm location until it has doubled in volume, about 1 hour.

Place the dough on a clean, dry, lightly floured work surface, using the remaining flour as necessary. Use a sharp knife to cut the dough into 12 equal portions. Shape each portion into a round ball. Divide the dough balls onto 2 baking sheets lined with parchment paper. Dust each dough ball with 1 teaspoon cornmeal. Allow to rise in a warm location until doubled in size, about 25 to 30 minutes.

Preheat the oven to 350°F.

Use a razor blade or a very sharp paring knife to cut a ¼-inch-deep slit into the top of each roll. Whisk together the egg yolk and 1 tablespoon cold water, then gently and lightly brush the top of each dough ball with this egg wash.

Bake the rolls for 25 to 30 minutes, rotating the sheets from top to bottom and front to back about halfway through the baking time.

Allow the rolls to cool thoroughly before cutting in half.

The rolls will keep fresh for 2 to 3 days stored in a resealable plastic bag at room temperature.

According to the oft-repeated tale of the origin of anadama bread, it was a New England fisherman's endearment—or perhaps his lack thereof—for his wife and her fondness for baking molasses bread that led to the epitaph "Anna was a lovely bride, but Anna, damn 'er, up and died." Apocryphal as this anecdote may be, this unique bread derives much character from molasses and cornmeal, and it is particularly good with Phyllis Flaherty-Bologna's burger.

Celeriac Chips

Yields 8 servings

2 pounds trimmed celery root (about 4 medium-size roots; see Note)
1 whole lemon, cut in half
6 cups vegetable oil
Salt and pepper to season

Using a sharp stainless steel paring knife, peel the outer skin from each celery root. Immediately rub each root with the cut end of a lemon half to prevent discoloration.

Using a mandoline or a very sharp stainless steel knife, slice the celery roots very thin, immediately placing the slices in ice water to prevent discoloration.

Heat the vegetable oil in a deep fryer (or high-sided. heavy-duty pot) fitted with a deep-frying basket over high heat to a temperature of 400°F. (In order to produce light, crispy, and greaseless chips, it is necessary to fry them at 400°F. The oil will probably need to be discarded after all of the chips for this recipe have been fried, as the high heat will shorten its life span.)

Drain the celery root slices in a colander and pat dry between paper towels.

Fry one-eighth the amount of the celery root slices until golden brown and crisp, about 1 to 1½ minutes. Transfer the fried slices to paper towels to drain. Repeat the frying procedure with the remaining batches of sliced celery root, waiting about 1 minute before frying each new batch to allow the oil to return to 400°F. Season with salt and pepper. Serve immediately.

The chips will keep warm and crisp in an oven set on warm for up to 2 hours. Do not salt the chips after they have been fried if you plan on keeping them in the oven; salt just before serving.

Note: Celeriac is known variously as celery root and knob celery. Purchase roots that are firm and have a clean and slightly celery-scented smell; avoid those that have a damp and musty aroma.

A typical medium-size celery root (trimmed of leaves and stalks) will weigh 8 to 10 ounces and be 3½ to 4 inches in diameter.

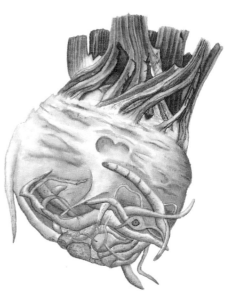

Filet of Beef Burger
with Yellow Corn Salsa

Makes 8 burgers

Larry Forgione
Chef/Owner
An American Place
New York, New York

HAILED AS ONE OF THE PIONEERS OF THE NEW AMERICAN CUISINE, LARRY FORGIONE HAS ESTABLISHED THE CRITERIA FOR INNOVATIVE YOUNG CULINARIANS IN THIS COUNTRY. HIS UNSTINTING USE OF AMERICAN INGREDIENTS HAS ENCOURAGED FARMSTEAD PRODUCERS TO GROW AND CULTIVATE A CONSTANTLY EXPANDING LIST OF UNIQUE AND DELECTABLE FOODS.

IN 1983, LARRY OPENED AN AMERICAN PLACE, WHICH FEATURES ONLY AMERICAN-GROWN AND -PRODUCED PRODUCTS. HE IS ALSO A PARTNER IN THE BEEKMAN 1766 TAVERN AT THE BEEKMAN ARMS IN RHINEBECK, NEW YORK, AND A CO-FOUNDER OF AMERICAN SPOON FOODS, A SPECIALTY FOOD COMPANY.

LARRY'S FILET OF BEEF BURGER IS A SOPHISTICATED VERSION OF AN AMERICAN FAVORITE.

Try a smooth Hudson Valley Lager Beer with Larry's burger.

1½ pounds lean beef tenderloin, cut into 1-inch pieces (or 1½ pounds ground lean beef tenderloin)

1 medium ripe avocado (6 to 7 ounces)

4 tablespoons American Spoon Foods barbecue sauce or other favorite sauce (see page 46 for Quick Barbecue Sauce)

2 tablespoons chopped fresh flat-leaf parsley

1 tablespoon chopped fresh cilantro

1 tablespoon olive oil

1 teaspoon salt

1 teaspoon freshly ground black pepper

8 Best Burger Buns (see page 109), cut in half

If using tenderloin pieces, grind through a meat grinder fitted with a coarse grinding plate into a 5-quart stainless steel bowl.

Cut, pit, and peel the avocado. Cut the avocado pulp into ⅛-inch pieces.

Gently but thoroughly combine the ground beef with the avocado pieces, barbecue sauce, parsley, cilantro, olive oil, salt, and pepper.

Gently form the meat-avocado mixture into eight 4-ounce, 1¼-inch-thick burgers. Cover the burgers with plastic wrap and refrigerate until needed.

Heat a well-seasoned flat griddle or a large nonstick sauté pan over medium-high heat. When hot, cook the burgers to the desired doneness: 3 to 4 minutes on each side for rare, 5 to 6 minutes on each side for medium, and 8 to 9 minutes on each side for well-done.

Toast the buns, cut side down, on the griddle or in a nonstick sauté pan until golden brown, about 1 minute. Serve the burgers on the toasted buns accompanied by Yellow Corn Salsa.

Yellow Corn Salsa

Yields 8 servings

4   large ears yellow sweet corn, husk and silk
    removed
2   jalapeño chiles, roasted, skinned, seeded, and
    minced
2   whole fresh limes
1   cup finely diced green bell peppers
1   cup finely diced red bell peppers
2   tablespoons chopped fresh cilantro
    Salt and freshly ground black pepper to
    season

Cook the corn for 4 minutes in 3 quarts boiling salted
water. Drain, then cool under cold running water. When
the corn is cool enough to handle, cut away the kernels.
Cover with plastic wrap and hold at room temperature
until needed.

In a 3-quart stainless steel bowl, combine the corn and
jalapeños. Cut the limes in half and squeeze the juice onto
the corn. Add the green bell peppers, red bell peppers, and
cilantro. Season with salt and freshly ground black pepper. Hold the salsa at room temperature covered with
plastic wrap for up to 2 hours before serving.

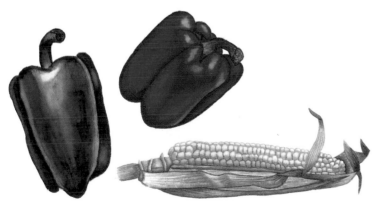

*The spirited tastes of this salsa seem
to be at their peak when it is freshly
prepared. It may, however, be made
in advance with a minimum loss of
flavor. Keep the salsa tightly covered
in the refrigerator for 2 to 3 days.
Allow it to stand at room temperature
for 30 to 40 minutes before serving
(the flavors of this mélange are
heightened by being served at room
temperature rather than chilled).*

*American Spoon Foods was founded
by Larry Forgione and his friend
Justin Rashid. Originally, many of
the products they sold, such as wild
berries, morel mushrooms, and
varietal honeys, were foraged for by
Rashid. Today, American Spoon
Foods sells a wide variety of products,
including award-winning preserves
as well as sauces and condiments
developed by Larry. If you are not
able to find these items in a specialty
store near you, they would be glad to
send you a catalog:*

*American Spoon Foods
P.O. Box 566
Petoskey, MI 49770
(800) 222-5886*

Virgin Island Codfish Burger
with Avocado and Tomato Relish and Okra Fungee

Makes 4 burgers

Jacqueline Frazer
Personal Caterer
New York, New York

WITH A DISTINCTIVE STYLE, VARIED MENUS, AND IMAGINATIVE PRESENTATIONS, JACQUELINE FRAZER IS ONE OF THE MOST SOUGHT-AFTER CHEFS FOR PRIVATE DINING AND BUSINESS ENTERTAINING IN THE NEW YORK METROPOLITAN AREA.

WITH A CLIENT LIST THAT REFLECTS NEW YORK'S MOVERS AND SHAKERS, JACQUELINE HAS SPENT HER YEARS SINCE GRADUATION PLEASING THE PALATES OF SUCH WELL-KNOWN PEOPLE AS LEONA AND HARRY HELMSLEY (SHE WAS THEIR PRIVATE CHEF IN 1986 AND 1987) AND, MORE RECENTLY, PUBLISHING MOGUL WILLIAM RANDOLPH HEARST, JR.

JACQUELINE'S VIRGIN ISLAND CODFISH BURGER IS A CONTEMPORARY INTERPRETATION OF A TRADITIONAL CARIBBEAN RECIPE FOR SALT CODFISH CAKES.

This codfish burger tantalizes the taste buds. Although the flavors are not bashful, they leave a subtle and pleasant taste lingering on the palate. Such interesting food calls for an equally appealing beverage. A cold ginger beer is great, but an even better suggestion is what Jacqueline calls an Island Manhattan—a couple of ounces of medium-dark rum and an ounce of sweet vermouth stirred with a few ice cubes.

2 teaspoons salt
1 small Idaho potato
1 pound fresh cod fillet, cut into 1/4-inch dice
1/2 cup minced onions
1 large egg, lightly beaten
2 scallions, trimmed and sliced thin
1 tablespoon chopped fresh parsley
1/2 teaspoon chopped fresh thyme
1/2 teaspoon dried red pepper flakes
1/4 teaspoon white pepper
1/2 cup olive oil
1/2 cup yellow cornmeal
8 small flour tortillas (see page 130; follow the recipe as directed, but omit the sage)

Heat 1 quart water with 1 teaspoon salt in a 2-quart saucepan over high heat. Peel the potato, then rinse with cold water. When the water boils, add the potato, adjust the heat, and allow the potato to simmer until cooked through, about 35 minutes. Remove the potato from the water, cut in half lengthwise, and cool uncovered in the refrigerator. When thoroughly cooled, grate the potato using a hand grater. Refrigerate until ready to assemble the burger.

In a 5-quart stainless steel bowl, gently but thoroughly combine the cod, grated potatoes, onions, egg, scallions, parsley, remaining 1 teaspoon salt, thyme, red pepper flakes, and pepper.

Gently form the cod mixture into four 6-ounce, 1-inch-thick burgers. Cover the burgers with plastic wrap and refrigerate until needed.

Preheat the oven to 400°F.

Heat the olive oil in a large nonstick sauté pan over medium-high heat. While the oil is heating, lightly coat the codfish burgers with the cornmeal. When the oil is hot, place the codfish burgers in the pan. Pan-fry the burgers until golden brown, about 2 minutes on each side. Transfer to a baking sheet and place in the oven until cooked through, about 10 minutes.

Cook the tortillas, 4 at a time, in a large nonstick sauté pan over medium-high heat until lightly browned, about 1 minute on each side.

Place each cod burger on a tortilla. Top each burger with 1 to 2 tablespoons Avocado and Tomato Relish and another tortilla. Serve accompanied by the Okra Fungee.

Avocado and Tomato Relish

Yields 1 1/4 cups

1   **medium avocado**
1   **small jalapeño chile, roasted, skinned, seeded, and minced**
1   **small ripe red tomato, peeled, seeded, and chopped**
1/4   **cup minced red onions**
1   **scallion, sliced thin**
2   **tablespoons extra-virgin olive oil**
1/2   **tablespoon chopped fresh parsley**
1   **teaspoon chopped fresh cilantro**
1/2   **teaspoon minced garlic**
    Juice of 1/2 lime
    Salt and pepper to season

Cut, pit, and peel the avocado. Cut the avocado halves into 1/4-inch pieces.

In a 3-quart stainless steel bowl, combine the avocado, jalapeños, tomatoes, red onions, scallions, olive oil, parsley, cilantro, and garlic. Add the lime juice, and season with salt and pepper. Use a rubber spatula to gently but thoroughly combine the mixture. Serve immediately. The Avocado and Tomato Relish may be kept covered in the refrigerator for several hours before serving.

> *This relish is a perfect condiment for Jacqueline's cod burger. No need to limit its use to the burger, however. It is wonderful with grilled fish and is an ideal accompaniment to a salad of grilled chicken breast with assorted greens and grilled red onions (brush the onions with olive oil and season liberally with salt and pepper before grilling).*

Okra Fungee

Yields 4 servings

1   **cup yellow cornmeal**
2 1/2   **cups cold water**
1 1/2   **teaspoons salt**
1/2   **teaspoon white pepper**
    Pinch cayenne pepper
1 1/4   **cups stemmed and sliced (1/4-inch-thick) fresh okra**
4   **tablespoons unsalted butter**

In a small stainless steel bowl, combine the cornmeal with 1 cup cold water.

Heat the remaining 1 1/2 cups water with the salt, white pepper, and cayenne pepper in a 2-quart saucepan over high heat. Bring to a boil, then add the okra and cook for 2 minutes. Add the cornmeal-water mixture. Bring the mixture to a boil, then reduce the heat to medium-low. Continue cooking, stirring constantly, until the mixture releases itself from the sides of the pan, about 3 to 4 minutes. Stir in the butter and serve immediately.

> *Okra Fungee, which Jacqueline fondly calls "Caribbean mashed potatoes," is an extraordinarily delicious recipe. Like polenta, Okra Fungee may be cooled, sliced, and pan-fried into a crisp and texturally intriguing item. For pan-fried Okra Fungee, cool the mixture on a baking sheet, spreading it out while it is still hot to a thickness of 1/2 to 3/4 inch. When the mixture is cool, cut it into 8 pieces, each 2 1/2 by 2 inches. Lightly brush a large nonstick sauté pan with olive oil. Heat the pan over medium-high heat. When the pan is hot, fry the Okra Fungee pieces for 2 1/2 to 3 minutes on each side. Serve hot and crisp.*

Flank Steak Chili Burger
with Smoky Cole Slaw and Black Bean Chili

Makes 6 burgers

Kevin Garvin
Executive Chef
The Adolphus Hotel
Dallas, Texas

KEVIN GARVIN, WHOSE TECHNIQUES WERE CALLED "SMART AND ENERGETIC" AND WHOSE ENTRÉES WERE DESCRIBED AS "DEVASTATINGLY DELICIOUS" IN A RECENT REVIEW, IS CUTTING A SWATH THROUGH THE FOOD WORLD OF DALLAS AND THE NATION.

WHEN THE *DALLAS MORNING NEWS* LISTED KEVIN AMONG THE YOUNG CHEFS TO WATCH IN THE 1990S, IT WAS HEDGING ITS BET. ALTHOUGH HE IS A YOUNG MAN, HIS YOUTH BELIES THE YEARS OF EXPERIENCE ALREADY UNDER HIS BELT.

BEFORE JOINING THE ADOLPHUS IN 1988, CHEF GARVIN HELD EXECUTIVE CHEF POSITIONS AT SEVERAL OTHER LUXURY HOTELS THROUGHOUT THE UNITED STATES. NOW ENSCONCED AT THE ADOLPHUS, KEVIN HAS DEVELOPED A CULINARY IDENTITY FOR THE HOTEL'S THREE RESTAURANTS. HE HAS ALSO EMERGED AS ONE OF DALLAS' MOST POPULAR TEACHING CHEFS.

IN MAY 1991, KEVIN WAS CHOSEN BY BUCKINGHAM PALACE TO PREPARE A PRIVATE LUNCHEON FOR HER MAJESTY QUEEN ELIZABETH II AND HIS ROYAL HIGHNESS PRINCE PHILIP, THE DUKE OF EDINBURGH.

BUT BACK HOME, KEVIN'S BURGER IMPARTS THE TRUE FLAVORS OF THE AMERICAN SOUTHWEST.

2 pounds flank steak, cut into ½-inch pieces (or 2 pounds ground flank steak)
1 teaspoon kosher salt
1 teaspoon ground cumin
¼ teaspoon cayenne pepper
3 tablespoons vegetable oil
1 tablespoon minced garlic
1 green bell pepper, seeded and diced
1 red bell pepper, seeded and diced
4 tablespoons masa harina (corn flour)
2 tablespoons all-purpose flour
 Salt and pepper to season
6 Best Burger Buns (see page 109), cut in half

If using flank steak pieces, grind through a meat grinder fitted with a coarse grinding plate into a 5-quart stainless steel bowl. Season the ground flank steak with the kosher salt, cumin, and cayenne pepper. Cover with plastic wrap and refrigerate until needed.

Heat 1 tablespoon vegetable oil in a medium nonstick sauté pan over medium-high heat. When hot, add the garlic and sauté for 30 seconds. Add the green bell peppers and red bell peppers, and continue to sauté until the peppers are tender, an additional 3 to 4 minutes, stirring frequently to avoid browning the garlic. Transfer the mixture to a dinner plate and place uncovered in the refrigerator to cool.

Add the cooled pepper-garlic mixture to the seasoned ground meat, and gently but thoroughly combine the ingredients.

Gently form the meat-pepper mixture into six 5- to 6-ounce, 1-inch-thick burgers. Cover the burgers with plastic wrap and refrigerate until needed.

Preheat the oven to 375°F.

Combine the masa harina and flour. Season with salt and pepper, and combine thoroughly.

Heat the remaining 2 tablespoons vegetable oil in a large nonstick sauté pan over medium-high heat. While the oil is heating, place the burgers into the masa harina–flour mixture; coat evenly and thoroughly. When the oil is hot, pan-fry the burgers in the vegetable oil, 3 at a time, until lightly browned, about 3 minutes on each side. Transfer to a baking sheet and place in the oven:

3 to 4 minutes for rare, 8 to 9 minutes for medium, and 10 to 12 minutes for well-done.

(If you prefer to grill the hamburgers, omit the masa harina–flour coating. Prior to grilling, season the burgers with salt and pepper. Grill the burgers over a medium wood or charcoal fire. Cook to the desired doneness: 3 to 4 minutes on each side for medium-rare, 5 to 6 minutes on each side for medium, and 8 to 9 minutes on each side for well-done.)

While the burgers are cooking, toast the buns in the oven until golden brown, about 3 to 4 minutes.

Place the burgers on the buns, top generously with Black Bean Chili, and serve accompanied by Smoky Cole Slaw.

Kevin Garvin also enjoys serving his Flank Steak Chili Burgers on multi-grain buns. Lone Star beer, brewed in Dallas, makes an appropriate beverage for Kevin's burger, no matter what bread it is served on. Or try a cold Shiner bock beer, brewed in Austin, Texas; this is Kevin's favorite.

Smoky Cole Slaw

Yields 4 cups

1   cup hickory wood chips
1   tablespoon grated fresh horseradish root
2   tablespoons cider vinegar
½   cup mayonnaise
3   scallions, trimmed and sliced thin diagonally
    Salt and pepper to season
¼   red cabbage, cored
¼   white cabbage, cored
3   medium carrots, peeled and split lengthwise
2   green peppers, split, stemmed, and seeded

Soak the hickory chips in cold water for at least 15 minutes. Drain well.

In a 3-quart stainless steel bowl, whisk together the horseradish, cider vinegar, mayonnaise, and scallions. Adjust the seasoning with salt and pepper, and combine thoroughly. Cover this dressing with plastic wrap and refrigerate until needed.

Prepare a small wood or charcoal fire in the grill. Allow the coals to mellow to a medium-low fire, then spread the coals evenly over the bottom of the grill. Sprinkle the soaked hickory chips onto the coals. While waiting for the chips to begin smoldering, arrange the vegetables on the grill rack. Place the rack with the vegetables on the grill. Cover the grill and smoke the vegetables for 15 to 20 minutes. (For a more profoundly smoky flavor, smoke the vegetables on the grill for an additional 5 to 10 minutes.)

Remove the vegetables from the grill and cool to room temperature.

Grate the vegetables in a food processor fitted with a medium grating disk.

Add the grated vegetables to the dressing, season with salt and pepper, and combine thoroughly. Serve the slaw immediately.

The slaw will keep tightly covered in the refrigerator for 1 to 2 days.

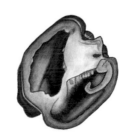

Black Bean Chili

Yields 2 cups

1 cup dried turtle beans, washed and picked over
1 tablespoon salt
1 tablespoon vegetable oil
2 small dried chipotle chiles, stemmed, seeded, and chopped (see Note)
½ cup tomato paste
2 tablespoons Ancho Paste (see following recipe)
2 tablespoons honey
Salt to season

Soak the black beans for 12 hours in 1 quart cold water. Drain the beans thoroughly before cooking.

Bring 2 quarts water and 1 tablespoon salt to a boil in a 5- or 6-quart saucepan over high heat. When the water boils, add the beans. Reduce the heat and simmer the beans until tender, about 30 minutes. Drain the cooked beans in a colander. Set aside until needed.

Heat the vegetable oil in a medium nonstick sauté pan over medium heat. When hot, add the chipotle chiles and sauté for 1 minute. Add the tomato paste and Ancho Paste, and cook, stirring constantly, for 3 minutes. Add the beans and honey. Season with salt. Continue to cook for 10 minutes. Serve immediately, or cool in an ice-water bath and refrigerate tightly covered for up to several days. When ready to reheat, add 1 to 2 tablespoons water and adjust the seasoning, if necessary. Serve hot.

Note: The distinctive smoky flavor of the chipotle chile lends a special undertone to this unusually delicious and easy-to-prepare chili. Look for this chile in specialty food stores.

Ancho Paste

Yields ¾ cup

1 medium jalapeño chile, roasted, skinned, and seeded
5 dried ancho chiles, stemmed and seeded (see Note)
½ cup chopped onions
1 clove garlic, peeled
1 cup water

Heat all the ingredients in a 2-quart saucepan over high heat. When the mixture comes to a boil, adjust the heat and allow to simmer until the ancho chiles are soft, about 15 minutes.

Puree the hot chile mixture in a food processor fitted with a metal blade until smooth. Strain the puree through a medium-gauge strainer. Use immediately, or cool to room temperature before refrigerating tightly covered in a noncorrosive container. The paste will keep in the refrigerator for several weeks.

Note: Although the deep red color of the ancho chile gives a murderous appearance to the paste, this chile is relatively mild in flavor. Look for ancho chiles in specialty food stores.

Salmon Burger
with Pernod, Mustard, and Dill Mayonnaise; Fennel and Red Onion Salad; and Sweet Potato Fries

Makes 4 burgers

John A. Halligan
Executive Chef
Rihga Royal Hotel
New York, New York

LANDMARK HOTELS HAVE BEEN JOHN HALLIGAN'S CULINARY PATH. AFTER GRADUATING FROM THE INSTITUTE, HE WENT TO WORK IN NEW YORK CITY AT THE REGENCY HOTEL ON PARK AVENUE, THEN THE HELMSLEY PARK LANE HOTEL ON CENTRAL PARK. IN 1988, JOHN OPENED THE EXCLUSIVE ST. JAMES'S CLUB AND HOTEL IN LOS ANGELES WHILE ALSO WORKING AS CONSULTANT TO THE OTHER ST. JAMES'S CLUBS IN PARIS, LONDON, AND ANTIGUA.

INSTEAD OF SPECIALIZING IN A SPECIFIC STYLE OF COOKING, JOHN STUDIES A WIDE VARIETY OF PREPARATION TECHNIQUES AND CUISINES. HE FEELS THAT TODAY'S FOOD SHOULD BE HEALTHY, ECLECTIC, IMAGINATIVE, UNRESTRICTED BY ETHNIC BOUNDARIES, AND ALWAYS EXPANDING; THIS PHILOSOPHY IS REFLECTED IN THE CUISINE AT THE RIHGA ROYAL HOTEL, ESPECIALLY THAT OF ITS HALCYON RESTAURANT.

JOHN'S SALMON BURGER ADDS QUITE A BIT OF SOPHISTICATION TO THIS ALL-AMERICAN FARE.

> *John recommends an exquisitely intense Chardonnay from Grgich Hills Cellars in Napa Valley. This relatively small winery produces some highly sought-after wines.*

20 ounces fresh salmon fillet, cut into ¼-inch dice
1 tablespoon Dijon mustard
1 tablespoon chopped fresh dill

Salt and pepper to season
8 slices Sesame Brioche (see page 60) or other favorite bread

In a 5-quart stainless steel bowl, gently but thoroughly combine the salmon, mustard, and dill. Liberally season with salt and pepper.

Gently form the salmon mixture into four 5-ounce, 1-inch-thick burgers. Cover the burgers with plastic wrap and refrigerate for at least 2 hours before using (the burgers must be refrigerated for the recommended time so that they will maintain their shape while cooking).

Heat a well-seasoned flat griddle or a large nonstick sauté pan over medium-high heat. When hot, cook the burgers for 3 to 5 minutes on each side, depending upon the preferred degree of doneness (3 minutes on each side will yield a medium-rare burger with a warm center; 5 minutes on each side will yield a burger that is cooked through).

Toast the brioche on the griddle or in a nonstick sauté pan until golden brown, about 1 minute.

Spread each slice of the brioche with a dollop of Pernod, Mustard, and Dill Mayonnaise. Serve the Salmon Burgers on the brioche immediately, each accompanied by a small ramekin of Pernod, Mustard, and Dill Mayonnaise, a serving of Fennel and Red Onion Salad, and lots of Sweet Potato Fries.

Pernod, Mustard, and Dill Mayonnaise

Yields ⅔ cup

½ cup mayonnaise
1 tablespoon Dijon mustard
1 teaspoon Pernod
½ teaspoon chopped fresh dill
   Salt and pepper to season

In a small stainless steel bowl, whisk together the mayonnaise, mustard, Pernod, and dill. Adjust the seasoning with salt and pepper, and combine thoroughly. Cover with plastic wrap and refrigerate until needed.

> *The distinct anise flavor of the Pernod in this recipe works well with the Salmon Burger and complements the Fennel and Red Onion Salad. Use the Pernod, Mustard, and Dill Mayonnaise with other bold-flavored fish dishes.*

Fennel and Red Onion Salad

Yields I quart

3 tablespoons red wine vinegar
2 tablespoons extra-virgin olive oil
2 tablespoons granulated sugar
1 tablespoon chopped fresh parsley
   Salt and pepper to season
2 medium fennel bulbs, cored and cut into long, thin strips (see Note)
1 medium red onion, sliced thin

In a 3-quart stainless steel bowl, whisk together the red wine vinegar, olive oil, sugar, and parsley. Season with salt and pepper.

Toss the fennel strips and red onion slices with the dressing. Adjust the seasoning with additional salt and pepper. Cover with plastic wrap and refrigerate for at least 2 hours before serving. The salad will keep tightly covered in the refrigerator for 2 to 3 days.

Note: Fennel, a totally engaging vegetable with a delicate licorice flavor that forms a long-lasting food memory, continues to find a wider audience. You will find fennel from October through February in produce markets and well-stocked supermarkets.

Cut the cored fennel bulb with a sharp stainless steel knife, or use a food processor fitted with a 4-millimeter slicing disk.

Sweet Potato Fries

Yields 4 servings

6 cups vegetable oil
4 medium sweet potatoes (about 8 ounces each), peeled
   Salt and pepper to season

Heat the vegetable oil in a deep fryer (or high-sided heavy-duty pot) fitted with a deep-frying basket over high heat to a temperature of 375°F.

Use a very sharp knife to slice the sweet potatoes into ⅛-inch-thick slices. Then cut the slices into ⅛-inch-thick strips. The potatoes may be deep-fried immediately or covered and refrigerated for up to 24 hours before frying.

Fry one-eighth the amount of sweet potatoes until lightly browned and crisp, about 1½ to 2 minutes. Transfer the fried sweet potatoes to paper towels to drain. Repeat the frying procedure with the remaining batches of raw sweet potato strips, waiting about 45 seconds before frying each new batch to allow the oil to return to 375°F. Season with salt and pepper. Serve immediately, or hold in a warm oven for up to 30 minutes before serving.

Provolone Ranger Burger
with Focaccia, Warm Olives and Tomatoes, and Fried Mozzarella

Makes 6 burgers

Stephanie Hersh
Julia Child Productions
Cambridge, Massachusetts

SINCE HER GRADUATION FROM THE CULINARY INSTITUTE OF AMERICA, STEPHANIE HERSH HAS HELD A NUMBER OF FOOD-RELATED JOBS IN THE BOSTON AREA. STEPHANIE IS CURRENTLY WORKING ON A MASTER'S DEGREE IN LIBERAL ARTS WITH A CONCENTRATION IN GASTRONOMY AT BOSTON UNIVERSITY, RUNNING A SMALL PASTRY/CATERING BUSINESS, AND TEACHING COOKING CLASSES TO PRESCHOOL CHILDREN AND CAKE-DECORATING CLASSES TO ADULTS. HER MOST EXCITING AND REWARDING POSITION IS AS JULIA CHILD'S FULL-TIME ASSISTANT.

STEPHANIE'S PROVOLONE RANGER BURGER WITH FRIED MOZZARELLA AND FOCACCIA DEMONSTRATES HOW SOPHISTICATED HER PALATE HAS GROWN SINCE THAT LONG-AGO SUMMER VACATION IN FLORIDA WHEN SHE AND HER FIVE COUSINS GORGED ON FAST-FOOD HAMBURGERS AT A GREAT NEW PLACE— BURGER KING. STEPHANIE NOSTALGICALLY REMEMBERS THE PROMOTIONAL SLOGAN THAT LURED HER AUNT AND UNCLE TO THIS NEW RESTAURANT: "THE BIGGER THE BURGER, THE BETTER THE BURGER; THE BURGERS ARE BIGGER AT BURGER KING!"

2	tablespoons vegetable oil	1	large egg, lightly beaten
1/4	cup minced onions	1 1/2	teaspoons salt
2	cloves garlic, minced	1	teaspoon pepper
2 1/2	pounds lean ground beef sirloin	6	1 1/2-ounce slices provolone cheese
1/4	cup bread crumbs	3	to 4 tablespoons olive oil
1/2	cup grated Romano cheese		

Heat the vegetable oil in a small nonstick sauté pan over medium heat. When hot, add the onions and sauté until tender, about 2 minutes. Reduce the heat to low, add the garlic, and cook for 1 minute. Remove the onions and garlic to a dinner plate, and place uncovered in the refrigerator to cool.

In a 5-quart stainless steel bowl, combine the chilled onion-garlic mixture with the ground beef. Add the bread crumbs, Romano, egg, salt, and pepper, and gently but thoroughly combine.

Gently form the meat mixture into six 7-ounce, 3/4-inch-thick burgers. Cover the burgers with plastic wrap and refrigerate until needed.

Grill the burgers over a medium wood or charcoal fire. Cook to the desired doneness: 3 to 4 minutes on each side for rare, 5 to 6 minutes on each side for medium, and 8 to 9 minutes on each side for well-done. Top each burger with a slice of the provolone and allow it to melt. If you have a cover for the grill, quickly melt the cheese by placing the cover over the grill for a few moments. (This burger may also be cooked on a well-seasoned flat griddle or in a large nonstick sauté pan over medium-high heat. Cook for about the same amount of time as listed for grilling.)

Remove the burgers from the grill. Brush 12 slices of Focaccia with the olive oil. Toast, oil side down, on the grill or griddle or in a nonstick sauté pan until golden brown, about 1 minute. Place each burger on a bottom half of Focaccia. Top each burger with Warm Olives and Tomatoes. Place a top half of Focaccia on each burger and serve with Fried Mozzarella.

Focaccia

Yields 8 servings

2	teaspoons granulated sugar
1¼	cups warm water
1	tablespoon active dry yeast
3½	cups all-purpose flour
8	tablespoons olive oil
1	teaspoon salt
1	tablespoon chopped fresh basil
2	teaspoons chopped fresh oregano
1	teaspoon kosher salt

In the bowl of an electric mixer, dissolve the sugar in ½ cup warm water. Add the yeast and stir gently to dissolve. Allow the mixture to stand and foam for 5 minutes.

Add the flour, 4 tablespoons olive oil, 1 teaspoon salt, and remaining ¾ cup warm water. Combine on the medium speed of an electric mixer fitted with a dough hook for 2 minutes. Scrape down the sides of the bowl, then continue to mix on low speed until the dough is smooth and elastic, about 5 to 6 minutes. If the dough forms a knot around the dough hook at any time, stop the mixer and remove the dough from the hook; continue mixing and repeat this procedure as necessary. (If a table-model electric mixer is not available, follow the directions using a hand-held mixer or kneading by hand. The mixing times will increase depending upon which alternative method is used.)

Remove the bowl from the mixer. Drizzle 1 tablespoon olive oil over the dough in the bowl and turn the dough several times to coat with the oil. Cover the bowl with a towel or plastic wrap. Allow the dough to rise in a warm location until doubled in volume, about 45 minutes.

Preheat the oven to 400°F.

Lightly coat a 15- by 10-inch baking sheet with sides with 1 tablespoon olive oil. Line the oiled baking sheet with parchment paper, then lightly coat the paper with an additional 1 tablespoon olive oil. Place the dough onto the baking sheet and flatten by hand into a rectangle measuring approximately 13 by 9 inches. Brush the top of the dough with the remaining 1 tablespoon olive oil. Sprinkle the basil, oregano, and kosher salt evenly over the dough.

Bake until lightly browned, 18 to 20 minutes.

Allow the Focaccia to cool to room temperature before cutting.

Remove the cooled Focaccia from the baking sheet. Cut in half lengthwise and then every 3¼ inches across the width. Cut each piece in half horizontally.

The Focaccia will keep fresh, stored in a resealable plastic bag, for 2 to 3 days at room temperature.

> *This bread is not only irresistible with the Provolone Ranger Burger but is also a fitting suitor to just about every burger in this book. For a light and delicious snack, try grilled Focaccia simply served with Warm Olives and Tomatoes. Add a glass of ripe and full-bodied Barolo.*

Warm Olives and Tomatoes

Yields 3 cups

1/4 cup extra-virgin olive oil
3 cloves garlic, minced
8 fresh plum tomatoes, cored and chopped
1/2 cup ripe olives, pitted and chopped
2 tablespoons chopped fresh basil
2 tablespoons balsamic vinegar
Salt and freshly ground black pepper to season

Heat the olive oil in a medium nonstick sauté pan over medium-low heat. When hot, add the garlic and sauté for 1 minute. Add the plum tomatoes and continue to sauté for 4 minutes. Remove from the heat and add the olives, basil, and balsamic vinegar. Season with salt and pepper. Serve immediately or cool in an ice-water bath. The cooled olives and tomatoes will keep in the refrigerator for a couple of days. Heat to a simmer before serving.

> *A few years back, Stephanie and her cousins preferred chocolate milk shakes with their burgers. Now the beverage of choice is a glass of Robert Mondavi Pinot Noir.*

Fried Mozzarella

Yields 6 servings

2 cups vegetable oil
2 large eggs
2 tablespoons cold water
6 1/2-inch-thick slices mozzarella cheese (about 2 ounces each; see Note)
1/2 cup all-purpose flour
1 1/2 cups dry bread crumbs
Salt and pepper to season

Heat the vegetable oil in a heavy frying pan over medium-high heat to a temperature of 375°F.

Whisk the eggs with the cold water until slightly foamy.

Dust the mozzarella slices with the flour and shake off any excess. Dip the slices into the beaten eggs and then into the bread crumbs, coating them evenly, lightly, and thoroughly.

Fry the cheese slices, 3 at a time, until golden brown and crispy, about 30 seconds on each side. Drain the fried cheese slices on paper towels, season with salt and pepper, and serve immediately.

Note: The mozzarella used for this recipe was cut into slices 4 inches long, 2 inches wide, and 1/2 inch thick.

> *This is a somewhat hefty but nonetheless quite comforting meal. To lighten things up a bit, serve the burger with Fennel and Red Onion Salad (see page 79) rather than with Fried Mozzarella.*

Spiced Pork Burger
with Ale and Onion Ragout and Carrot and Scallion Salad

Makes 6 burgers

James Heywood
Chef-Instructor
The Culinary Institute of America
Hyde Park, New York

WILL ANY GOOD COME FROM
SPECULATING WHERE JIM HEYWOOD
PICKED UP THE NICKNAME "HOG BREATH"?
SUFFICE IT TO SAY THAT THIS BELOVED
TEACHER REVELS IN ANY AND ALL
PRESUMPTIONS AS TO THE GENESIS OF THAT
MONIKER. ALTHOUGH CHEF HEYWOOD IS
RENOWNED FOR HIS FAMOUS CHILI RECIPE,
HAVING BEEN BOTH A CONTESTANT AND A
JUDGE AT SOME OF THE MOST PRESTIGIOUS
CHILI COMPETITIONS THROUGHOUT THE
NATION, HIS SPICED PORK BURGER RECIPE
SHOULD ENSURE THAT KUDOS RATHER
THAN NICKNAMES COME HIS WAY.

This substantial burger should be approached with knife and fork in hand. Serve any remaining ragout as a side dish, or save for a subsequent burger attack.

2¼ pounds trimmed fresh pork butt, cut into 1-inch pieces (or 2¼ pounds ground trimmed pork butt)
1 tablespoon unsalted butter
4 tablespoons finely chopped shallots
1 clove garlic, finely minced
4 tablespoons chopped fresh parsley
2 teaspoons salt
1 teaspoon freshly ground black pepper
pinch rubbed sage
pinch celery seeds
pinch ground mace
pinch cayenne pepper
6 Onion Rolls (see page 89), cut in half
½ pound coarsely grated cheddar cheese

If using pork pieces, grind through a chilled meat grinder fitted with a coarse grinding plate into a 5-quart stainless steel bowl. Cover with plastic wrap and refrigerate until needed.

Heat the butter in a small nonstick sauté pan over medium heat. When the butter is hot, add shallots and garlic, and sauté for 2 minutes. Remove shallots and garlic to a dinner plate, and place uncovered in the refrigerator to cool.

Combine the chilled shallot-garlic mixture with the ground pork. Add the parsley, salt, ground black pepper, sage, celery seeds, mace, and cayenne pepper. Gently but thoroughly combine the ingredients.

Gently form the meat mixture into six 6-ounce, 1-inch-thick burgers. Cover the burgers with plastic wrap and refrigerate until needed.

Preheat the oven to 300°F.

Heat a well-seasoned flat griddle or a large nonstick sauté pan over medium heat. When hot, cook the burgers for 2 to 3 minutes on each side. Place the burgers on a baking sheet in the oven until cooked medium, about 15 to 16 minutes. Remove the burgers from the oven.

Toast the rolls, cut side down, on the griddle or a nonstick sauté pan over medium-high heat until golden brown, about 1 minute.

Portion 2 tablespoons hot Ale and Onion Ragout onto the bottom half of each toasted roll. Place a burger on each ragout-covered roll. Evenly divide the cheddar over the burgers. Top with the other halves of the toasted rolls, and serve immediately with Carrot and Scallion Salad and Chef Heywood's recommended brew: Genesee 12 Horse Ale.

Ale and Onion Ragout

Yields 6 servings

2	tablespoons unsalted butter
2	teaspoons Hungarian paprika
2	medium onions, sliced 1/8 inch thick
2	cloves garlic, minced
5	tablespoons all-purpose flour
1/2	cup chicken stock, hot
3	tablespoons ketchup
1	tablespoon coarse-ground whole-seed mustard
1 1/2	cups ale or beer
	Salt and pepper to season

Melt the butter in a 2 1/2-quart saucepan over medium-high heat. When hot, add the paprika and constantly stir for 2 minutes. Add the onions and garlic, and sauté, stirring frequently, until the onions are translucent, about 10 to 12 minutes. Reduce the heat to medium.

Add the flour. Cook for 3 to 4 minutes, stirring constantly to prevent browning or scorching.

Add the hot chicken stock, ketchup, and mustard. Stir the mixture constantly until thickened and smooth, about 6 to 8 minutes.

Add the ale or beer, and stir to incorporate. Bring the ragout to a boil, then lower the heat and allow to simmer for 15 to 20 minutes. Adjust the seasoning with salt and pepper.

Serve Ale and Onion Ragout hot over Spiced Pork Burgers.

This ragout may be cooled in an ice-water bath, then stored covered in the refrigerator for several days. Heat the ragout to a boil before serving.

Carrot and Scallion Salad

Yields 6 servings

1 1/2	teaspoons salt
2	pounds carrots, peeled and ends trimmed
1/4	cup distilled white vinegar
6	tablespoons vegetable oil
1/2	tablespoon prepared Creole mustard (see Note)
1/2	tablespoon honey
1/2	tablespoon chopped fresh dill
1/2	tablespoon chopped fresh parsley
1/2	teaspoon white pepper
6	scallions, trimmed and sliced thin diagonally

Bring 2 quarts water and 1 teaspoon salt to a boil in a 4-quart saucepan over high heat. Cook the carrots in the boiling water until tender, about 14 to 15 minutes. Drain the carrots, then plunge into ice water. When the carrots are thoroughly cooled, remove from the ice water and drain well. Cut the cooled carrots into 1/8-inch-thick diagonal slices.

In a 3-quart stainless steel bowl, whisk together the white vinegar, vegetable oil, mustard, honey, dill, and parsley. Add the remaining 1/2 teaspoon salt and the pepper, and combine thoroughly. Add the carrots and scallions, and toss gently to combine. The salad can be kept tightly covered in a noncorrosive container in the refrigerator for 3 to 4 days.

Note: Jim recommends Zatarain's Creole mustard for his Carrot and Scallion Salad. If Creole mustard is not available, use your favorite spicy mustard.

Veal and Smoked Gouda Burger
with Creamy Mustard-Dill Potato Salad

Makes 6 burgers

Liz Heywood
Chef-Instructor
The Culinary Institute of America
Hyde Park, New York

CHEF LIZ HEYWOOD DID NOT VENTURE FAR FROM THE INSTITUTE FOLLOWING GRADUATION. RATHER, SHE CHOSE TO DO A FELLOWSHIP (IN EFFECT TO BECOME A TEACHER'S ASSISTANT) IN THE HIGHLY TOUTED ESCOFFIER RESTAURANT AT THE INSTITUTE. SHE THEN WORKED AS SOUS CHEF AT THE BEEKMAN ARMS IN RHINEBECK, NEW YORK, UNTIL 1978, WHEN SHE STARTED COUNTRY BUFFET, A CATERING AND SPECIALTY BAKING OPERATION.

LIZ IS PRESENTLY A CHEF-INSTRUCTOR AT THE CULINARY INSTITUTE, AND SHE IS STILL RUNNING THE CATERING BUSINESS IN HER SPARE TIME.

LIZ'S VEAL AND SMOKED GOUDA BURGER CARRIES THE SAME COUNTRY FLAIR THAT IS A TRADEMARK OF HER CATERING FIRM.

> *The absence of a sauce or condiment to dress the burger may tempt one to reach for a ketchup bottle. Although this is not verboten, it is not encouraged, since the cheese and the potato salad provide a creamy contrast for this already juicy burger.*

1 tablespoon olive oil
1/2 cup finely diced onions
1 green apple (Granny Smith)
1 teaspoon minced garlic
4 tablespoons chopped fresh parsley
2 teaspoons salt
1 teaspoon chopped fresh oregano
1 teaspoon chopped fresh sage
3/4 teaspoon freshly ground black pepper
1 1/2 pounds ground veal
4 ounces diced pork fat
6 1/2-ounce slices smoked Gouda cheese
6 Onion Rolls (see page 89), cut in half
1 large bunch watercress, stems trimmed, washed, and dried

Heat the olive oil in a medium nonstick sauté pan over medium heat. When hot, add the onions and sauté until lightly browned, about 10 minutes. While the onions are cooking, core and dice the apple (do not peel). Add the diced apple and garlic to the lightly browned onions, and sauté for 2 minutes. Add the parsley, salt, oregano, sage, and pepper, and stir to combine. Transfer the onion-apple mixture to a dinner plate, and place uncovered in the refrigerator to cool.

In a 5-quart stainless steel bowl, gently but thoroughly combine the ground veal, cooled onion-apple mixture, and pork fat.

Gently form the meat mixture into six 6-ounce, 1-inch-thick burgers. Cover the burgers with plastic wrap and refrigerate until needed.

Preheat the oven to 325°F.

Heat a well-seasoned flat griddle or a large nonstick sauté pan over medium-high heat. When hot, cook the burgers for 2 minutes on each side. Transfer the burgers to a baking sheet with sides and finish cooking in the oven: 8 to 10 minutes for medium and 10 to 12 minutes for medium-well. Remove the burgers from the oven and top each with a slice of the smoked Gouda.

Toast the roll halves on the griddle or in a nonstick sauté pan over medium-high heat until golden brown, about 1 minute. Serve the Veal and Smoked Gouda Burgers immediately on the toasted buns accompanied by Creamy Mustard-Dill Potato Salad and garnished with the watercress sprigs.

Creamy Mustard-Dill Potato Salad

Yields 6 servings

2½   **pounds red bliss potatoes (washed but not peeled)**
    Salt and pepper to season
1   **tablespoon whole mustard seeds**
4   **tablespoons red wine vinegar**
2   **tablespoons Dijon mustard**
1   **tablespoon mayonnaise**
2   **tablespoons chopped fresh dill**
1   **tablespoon chopped fresh parsley**
1   **tablespoon minced shallots**
1   **clove garlic, minced**
1   **teaspoon granulated sugar**
¼   **teaspoon Worcestershire sauce**
1   **cup safflower or vegetable oil**
½   **cup extra-virgin olive oil**

Place the potatoes in a 6-quart pot and cover with cold water. Bring to a simmer over medium-high heat, then adjust the heat and allow to simmer slowly until potatoes are tender, about 20 to 22 minutes. Drain the hot water from the potatoes, then cool under slowly running cold water until cool to the touch. Refrigerate the potatoes for 30 minutes. Slice the chilled potatoes into ¼-inch-thick slices. Lightly season the sliced potatoes with salt and pepper.

Preheat the oven to 375°F.

Toast the mustard seeds on a baking sheet with sides in the oven for 2 minutes. Allow to cool.

Prepare the dressing in a 5-quart stainless steel bowl by whisking together the red wine vinegar, mustard, and mayonnaise. Add the dill, parsley, shallots, garlic, sugar, Worcestershire sauce, and toasted mustard seeds. Continue to whisk the mixture while adding a slow, steady stream of the safflower or vegetable oil, then the olive oil. Adjust the seasoning with salt and pepper, and combine thoroughly.

Gently toss the potato slices with the dressing. Cover the bowl with plastic wrap and refrigerate for 2 to 3 hours before serving. The salad will keep covered in the refrigerator for 2 days.

> *This salad is liberally dressed intentionally. For a lighter salad, the dressing recipe may be cut in half, resulting in a less viscous yet still pleasing potato salad.*

> *A first-rate Seyval Blanc from Clinton Vineyards in Clinton Corners, New York, is Liz's recommended wine.*

Sally's Famous Hamburger
with Onion Rolls

Makes 4 burgers

Gerry Klaskala

Chef/Managing Partner
The Buckhead Diner
Atlanta, Georgia

ARGUABLY ATLANTA'S MOST POPULAR RESTAURANT, THE BUCKHEAD DINER ALMOST ALWAYS HAS A CLUSTER OF HUNGRY PATRONS WAITING TO BE SEATED. THIS IS DUE TO THE FACT THAT GERRY KLASKALA IS AHEAD OF HIS COMPETITION IN THAT MAGIC COMBINATION OF EDUCATION, TRAINING, CREATIVITY, AND SKILLS, WHICH ENABLES HIM TO PREPARE THE DELICIOUS FOOD HIS CUSTOMERS HAVE COME TO EXPECT.

HOWEVER, AFTER A HARD WEEK AT THE DINER, GERRY IS LIKELY TO BE FOUND RELAXING WHILE HIS WIFE, SALLY, DOES THE COOKING. ALTHOUGH SALLY IS NOT AN ALUMNA OF THE INSTITUTE, SHE PRIDES HERSELF ON MAKING A GREAT HAMBURGER.

PROFESSIONALLY SPEAKING, THESE BURGERS ARE DELICIOUS.

Gerry encourages you to embellish Sally's burger with a slice or two of your favorite cheese. Also de rigueur with burgers at Gerry and Sally's house is a bottle of Heinz ketchup and a jar of Weber's horseradish mustard from Buffalo, New York. And don't forget some cold beer; at the Klaskalas' it will probably be Helen bock beer from Helen, Georgia.

1½   pounds ground beef chuck
1   cup minced onions
½   cup dry bread crumbs
1   large egg, lightly beaten
1   tablespoon prepared mustard
2   teaspoons Worcestershire sauce
1   teaspoon prepared horseradish
1   teaspoon chopped fresh oregano
     Salt and pepper to season
4   tablespoons mayonnaise
4   iceberg lettuce leaves, washed and dried
     Spiced Tomato Relish (see page 38)

In a 5-quart stainless steel bowl, place the ground beef, onions, bread crumbs, egg, mustard, Worcestershire sauce, horseradish, and oregano. Season with salt and pepper, and gently but thoroughly combine.

Gently form the mixture into four 8-ounce, 1¼-inch-thick burgers. Cover the burgers with plastic wrap and refrigerate until needed.

Grill the burgers over a medium wood or charcoal fire. Cook to the desired doneness: 4 to 5 minutes on each side for rare, 6 to 7 minutes on each side for medium, and 9 to 10 minutes on each side for well-done. (This burger may also be cooked on a well-seasoned flat griddle or in a large nonstick sauté pan over medium-high heat. Cook for about the same amount of time as listed for grilling.)

Cut 4 Onion Rolls in half. Toast the Onion Rolls, cut side down, on the grill or griddle or in a nonstick sauté pan until golden brown, about 1 minute.

Spread the top half of each roll with 1 tablespoon mayonnaise. Place a burger on the bottom half of each toasted roll. Top each burger with 1 of the lettuce leaves, 1 to 2 tablespoons Spiced Tomato Relish, and a top roll half.

Onion Rolls

Makes 12 rolls

- **¼ cup plus 2 tablespoons and 1 teaspoon olive oil**
- **3 cups thinly sliced onions**
- **2½ teaspoons salt**
- **¼ teaspoon cracked black pepper**
- **1 tablespoon granulated sugar**
- **1¾ cups warm water**
- **2 tablespoons active dry yeast**
- **6½ cups bread flour**

Heat ¼ cup olive oil in a 2½-quart saucepan over medium heat. When hot, add the onions, ½ teaspoon salt, and pepper. Cover the pan, and cook until the onions are translucent, about 10 minutes. Transfer the onions to a dinner plate and hold uncovered at room temperature until needed.

In the bowl of an electric mixer, dissolve the sugar in ½ cup warm water. Add the yeast and stir gently to dissolve. Allow the mixture to stand and foam for 5 to 6 minutes.

Place the mixing bowl on an electric mixer fitted with a dough hook. On top of the yeast mixture, add 6 cups flour, the remaining 1¼ cups warm water, ½ cup cooked onions, 2 tablespoons olive oil, and the remaining 2 teaspoons salt. Mix on low speed for 1 minute, then scrape down the sides of the bowl. Continue to mix on low speed for an additional minute, then scrape down the sides of the bowl. Adjust the mixer speed to medium-low, and mix until the dough is smooth and elastic, about 3 to 4 minutes. (If a table-model electric mixer is not available, follow the directions using a hand-held mixer or kneading by hand. The mixing times will increase depending upon which alternative method is used.)

Remove the bowl from the mixer. Drizzle the remaining 1 teaspoon olive oil over the dough in the bowl, and turn the dough several times to coat with the oil. Cover the dough with a towel or plastic wrap. Allow the dough to rise in a warm location until doubled in size, about 45 minutes.

Preheat the oven to 325°F.

When the dough has doubled in size, punch it down to its original size. Once again cover with a towel or plastic wrap and allow to double in size for a second time, about 30 minutes.

Place the dough on a clean, dry, lightly floured work surface, using the remaining ½ cup flour as necessary. Use a sharp knife to cut the dough into 12 equal portions. Shape each portion of dough into a smooth ball. Divide the dough balls onto 2 baking sheets lined with parchment paper. Loosely cover each baking sheet of rolls with plastic wrap. Allow the rolls to rise in a warm location until doubled in size, about 35 to 40 minutes. Slightly flatten the top of each roll using your fingertips. Equally divide the remaining cooked onions onto the rolls, spreading evenly over the tops. Bake the rolls until they are golden in color and the onions are caramelized, about 35 to 40 minutes.

Allow the rolls to cool thoroughly before slicing them horizontally.

The rolls will keep fresh for 2 to 3 days at room temperature stored in a resealable plastic bag.

> *These versatile rolls not only will complement virtually every burger in this book, they also are terrific for sandwiches. Try your favorite sandwich on Gerry's Onion Roll—and you may just find yourself baking as many as they do at The Buckhead Diner—well, almost!*

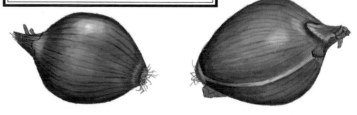

Hamburger à la Lindstrom
with Mounds of Golden Crisp-Fried Onions and Dilled Sour Cream

Makes 4 burgers

Jenifer Lang
Managing Director/Owner
Café des Artistes
New York, New York

A SELF-PROCLAIMED "FOOD FREAK" AS
WELL AS AN ACCOMPLISHED JOURNALIST,
JENIFER LANG ENROLLED AT THE CULINARY
INSTITUTE IN ORDER TO ENHANCE HER
SKILLS WITH A PROFESSIONAL CHEF'S
TRAINING.

AFTER GRADUATING FROM THE
INSTITUTE, JENIFER BECAME CHEF AT
NATHANS IN GEORGETOWN. SINCE 1990,
SHE HAS BEEN THE MANAGING DIRECTOR
OF THE THREE-STAR CAFÉ DES ARTISTES.
JENIFER CONTINUES TO WRITE, AND SHE
MAKES FREQUENT APPEARANCES ON
NATIONAL TELEVISION. HER ARTICLES ON
FOOD, RESTAURANTS, AND CONSUMER
SUBJECTS APPEAR IN MANY NATIONAL
FOOD AND GENERAL-INTEREST
MAGAZINES.

THIS SCANDINAVIAN-INSPIRED
HAMBURGER À LA LINDSTROM IS A MEAL
IN ITSELF, WITH MEAT, POTATO, AND
VEGETABLE ALL TOGETHER. JENIFER
ORIGINALLY DEVISED IT FOR HER SON,
SIMON, AS A WAY TO SNEAK VEGETABLES
INTO HIS BURGERS.

1	tablespoon unsalted butter
¹/₄	cup minced onions
¹/₂	cup peeled and diced fresh beets (¹/₄-inch dice)
2	teaspoons salt
¹/₂	cup peeled and diced Idaho potatoes (¹/₄-inch dice)
1¹/₄	pounds lean ground beef chuck
	Salt and freshly ground black pepper to season
4	Onion Rolls (see page 89) or other favorite rolls, cut in half

Heat the butter in a small nonstick sauté pan over medium-high heat. When the butter is hot, sauté the onions until tender, about 2 to 3 minutes. Transfer the onions to a dinner plate and place uncovered in the refrigerator to cool.

In a 2-quart saucepan, cover the beets with 2 cups water salted with 1 teaspoon salt. Cook over medium-high heat, bringing the water to a simmer. Adjust the heat and continue to simmer slowly until the beets are thoroughly cooked yet still firm, about 10 to 15 minutes. Drain the cooked beets, then transfer to a dinner plate and cool uncovered in the refrigerator.

In a 2-quart saucepan, cover the potatoes with 2 cups water salted with the remaining 1 teaspoon salt. Cook over medium-high heat, bringing the water to a simmer. Adjust the heat and continue to simmer slowly until potatoes are cooked but still firm, about 7 to 8 minutes. Drain the cooked potatoes, then transfer to a dinner plate and cool uncovered in the refrigerator.

In a 5-quart stainless steel bowl, gently but thoroughly combine the ground beef, onions, beets, and potatoes.

Gently form the ground beef mixture into four 7-ounce, 1-inch-thick burgers. Season with salt and pepper. Cover the burgers with plastic wrap and refrigerate until needed.

Heat a well-seasoned flat griddle or a large nonstick sauté pan over medium-high heat. When hot, cook the burgers for 3 to 4 minutes on each

A recipe for Hamburger à la Lindstrom appeared in Jenifer's best-selling Jenifer Lang Cooks for Kids. *The recipe was revised for this book with grown-up kids in mind.*

side for rare, 5 to 6 minutes on each side for medium, and 8 to 9 minutes on each side for well-done.

Toast the roll halves, cut side down, on the griddle or in a nonstick sauté pan until golden brown, about 1 minute.

Serve each burger, topped with 1 to 2 tablespoons Dilled Sour Cream, on a toasted roll, accompanied by Mounds of Golden Crisp-Fried Onions.

Mounds of Golden Crisp-Fried Onions

Yields 4 generous servings

6 **cups vegetable oil**
1½ **cups all-purpose flour**
2 **tablespoons freshly ground black pepper**
2 **teaspoons salt**
2 **large onions, cut in half, cores removed, and sliced thin**
Salt and pepper to season

Heat the vegetable oil in a deep fryer (or high-sided, heavy-duty pot) over high heat to a temperature of 350°F.

In a 5-quart stainless steel bowl, thoroughly combine the flour, freshly ground black pepper, and 2 teaspoons salt.

Toss the sliced onions in the seasoned flour. Coat the onions evenly, lightly, and thoroughly. Shake off excess flour.

Fry one-fourth the amount of onions until golden brown and crispy, about 2 minutes. Use a skimmer or a large slotted spoon to transfer the fried onions to paper towels to drain. Repeat the frying procedure with the remaining batches of onions, waiting about 2 minutes before frying each new batch to allow the oil to return to 350°F. Season with salt and pepper. Serve immediately.

The onions will keep warm and crispy in a warm oven for up to 30 minutes.

Dilled Sour Cream

Yields ½ cup

½ **cup sour cream**
2 **tablespoons minced red onions**
1 **teaspoon chopped fresh dill**
Salt and pepper to season

In a small stainless steel bowl, combine the sour cream, red onions, and dill. Use a rubber spatula to blend the mixture. Adjust the seasoning with salt and pepper, and combine thoroughly. Serve immediately, or keep tightly covered in the refrigerator for 2 to 3 days.

Lentil Walnut Burger

with Ginger Yogurt Dressing, Vinegar Greens, and Basmati Rice with Vegetable Confetti

Makes 6 burgers

Daniel Leader
Owner/Baker
Bread Alone
Boiceville, New York

BUILDING A WOOD-FIRED BRICK OVEN WAS NOT PART OF THE CURRICULUM AT THE CULINARY INSTITUTE WHEN DAN LEADER WAS THERE. BUT EVEN THEN, HE HAD A PASSION FOR BREAD-BAKING—SPECIFICALLY TRADITIONAL EUROPEAN HEARTH-BAKED BREADS. SO FOLLOWING GRADUATION, DAN TRAVELED EXTENSIVELY IN EUROPE, STUDYING TRADITIONAL METHODS OF BREAD-BAKING AND LEARNING TO BUILD A WOOD-FIRED BRICK OVEN. AT HIS BAKERY, BREAD ALONE, DAN HAS WOOD-FIRED BRICK OVENS THAT HE BUILT HIMSELF.

DAN LEADER'S BURGER IS EXEMPLARY OF THE WHOLESOME APPROACH HE TAKES TO LIFE AND HIS CRAFT.

French green lentils, specifically those labeled La Lentille Verte du Puy, *simply have no peers. These fine little beans have delicate skins, a firm texture, and a nutty flavor. Grown in volcanic-enriched soil, they are loaded with nutritionally beneficial components and are worth their price; in fact, no other lentil will work as well in this recipe.*

2 cups French green lentils, picked over, washed, and drained
2 teaspoons salt
3 tablespoons safflower or vegetable oil
1/2 cup minced onions
2 teaspoons minced garlic
1 teaspoon grated fresh ginger
3/4 cup chopped toasted walnuts
Salt and pepper to season
6 whole wheat pita breads

Place the lentils in a 2-quart saucepan, cover with 1 quart cold water and 2 teaspoons salt, and bring to a simmer. Adjust the heat to simmer the lentils slowly until cooked, about 20 to 25 minutes. Drain the cooked lentils in a colander. Transfer the lentils to a large plate or platter, and keep uncovered in the refrigerator to cool.

Heat 1 tablespoon safflower or vegetable oil in a small nonstick sauté pan over medium high heat. When hot, add the onions, garlic, and ginger, and sauté until tender, about 2 to 3 minutes. Transfer the onion mixture to a dinner plate and place uncovered in the refrigerator to cool.

Puree 1/2 cup walnuts in a food processor fitted with a metal blade.

In a 5-quart stainless steel bowl, gently but thoroughly combine the cooled lentils, chilled onion mixture, remaining 1/4 cup walnuts, and walnut puree. Season with salt and pepper.

Form the lentil mixture into six 5-ounce, 3/4-inch-thick burgers. Cover the burgers with plastic wrap and refrigerate until needed.

Preheat the oven to 350°F.

Heat the remaining 2 tablespoons safflower or vegetable oil in a large nonstick sauté pan over medium-high heat. When hot, sauté the burgers until lightly browned, about 2 minutes on each side. Transfer the burgers to a baking sheet and place in the oven for 8 to 10 minutes. About 1 to 2 minutes before burgers are finished cooking, place the pita breads on a baking sheet in the oven to warm.

Remove the pita breads and burgers from the oven. Cut a 1 3/4-inch piece from the top of each pita bread, and gently split open the bread. Stuff each pita with a Lentil Walnut Burger, and spoon 2 to 3 teaspoons Ginger Yogurt Dressing directly on the meat. Serve burgers accompanied by Vinegar Greens and Basmati Rice with Vegetable Confetti.

93

Ginger Yogurt Dressing

Yields 1 cup

1 cup lowfat yogurt
1 tablespoon grated fresh ginger
1 teaspoon chopped fresh parsley
  Salt and pepper to season

In a small stainless steel bowl, combine the yogurt, ginger, and parsley. Season with salt and pepper, and combine thoroughly. Serve immediately, or refrigerate tightly covered for up to 3 to 4 hours before serving.

Vinegar Greens

Yields 6 servings

2 tablespoons safflower or vegetable oil
2 tablespoons water
3 bunches Swiss or ruby chard, stemmed, washed, dried, and torn into 2- to 3-inch pieces (see Note)
1 tablespoon balsamic vinegar
  Freshly ground black pepper to season

Heat the safflower or vegetable oil and water in a large nonstick sauté pan over medium-high heat. When hot, add the chard. Steam the greens until hot and wilted, about 3 to 4 minutes. Remove from the heat, and finish by splashing the chard with the balsamic vinegar and with a twist or two of pepper. Serve immediately.

Note: If chard is not available, use whatever seasonal greens look fresh and salubrious, such as mustard greens, turnip greens, curly kale, or collard greens.

The flavor of this dressing is at its peak when freshly prepared. Dan suggests that you prepare it as close to serving time as possible. Dan also makes a point of using fresh ginger, since its pure, spicy flavor simply has no substitute.

Basmati Rice with Vegetable Confetti

Yields 6 servings

2 tablespoons olive oil
3/4 cup finely diced carrots
3/4 cup finely diced red onions
1/3 cup finely diced celery
1/3 cup finely diced red peppers
  Salt and white pepper to season
1 1/2 cups white basmati rice (see Note)
3 cups water or vegetable stock, hot

Heat the olive oil in a 4-quart saucepan over medium-high heat. When hot, add the carrots, red onions, celery, and red peppers. Season with salt and pepper, and sauté for 4 to 5 minutes. Add the rice and stir to combine thoroughly. Then add the hot water or vegetable stock. Adjust the heat to high and bring to a boil. As soon as the liquid boils, cover the saucepan and reduce the heat to medium. Allow the rice to cook undisturbed until tender, about 12 to 15 minutes. Remove the saucepan from the heat. Serve the rice immediately, or hold covered, away from the heat, for up to 45 minutes.

Note: Delicious basmati rice is so easily prepared that it is surprising it is not more popular. Although grown in several areas of the world, the soil of northern India seems to produce the finest example of this unique grain. Look for white or brown basmati rice in specialty grocery stores and health food stores as well as in well-stocked major supermarkets.

Veal and Apricot Burger

with Honey Mustard Cream and Apple and Walnut Salad

Makes 4 burgers

Vinnie Oakes

Vice President of Food and Beverage
Desert Inn Hotel and Country Club
Las Vegas, Nevada

WHEN HE GRADUATED FROM THE CULINARY INSTITUTE OF AMERICA, VINNIE OAKES KNEW THAT HIS FOOD-SERVICE CAREER WOULD TAKE HIM BEYOND THE KITCHEN. TO PREPARE FOR THE OPPORTUNITIES IN MANAGEMENT, VINNIE ATTENDED THE UNIVERSITY OF DENVER, MAJORING IN HOTEL AND RESTAURANT MANAGEMENT. HE GRADUATED IN 1969 WITH A BACHELOR OF SCIENCE DEGREE IN BUSINESS ADMINISTRATION.

AFTER GRADUATION FROM THE UNIVERSITY OF DENVER, VINNIE WORKED FOR THE LEGENDARY GEORGE LANG AT RESTAURANT ASSOCIATES. HE LATER JOINED HARRAH'S HOTEL AND CASINO AS DIRECTOR OF FOOD OPERATIONS AND THEN BECAME DIRECTOR OF THE FOOD DIVISION FOR SILVER DOLLAR CITY THEME PARK IN BRANSON, MISSOURI. VINNIE IS PRESENTLY VICE PRESIDENT OF FOOD AND BEVERAGE AT THE DESERT INN HOTEL AND COUNTRY CLUB IN LAS VEGAS.

VINNIE'S BURGER IS PROOF THAT YOU CAN TAKE A CULINARY GRADUATE OUT OF THE KITCHEN BUT YOU CANNOT TAKE THE KITCHEN OUT OF HIS PSYCHE. VINNIE BASED THIS BURGER ON THE TRADITIONAL DANISH MEAT PATTY CALLED *FRIKADELLER*.

12 ounces lean veal, cut into 1-inch pieces (or 12 ounces ground lean veal)

8 ounces trimmed pork butt, cut into 1-inch pieces (or 8 ounces ground trimmed pork butt)

$^1/_2$ cup minced onions

$^1/_4$ cup minced dried apricots

1 teaspoon salt

$^1/_2$ teaspoon white pepper

$^1/_4$ teaspoon finely chopped fresh rosemary

8 slices Jewish rye bread

If using veal and pork pieces, grind through a meat grinder fitted with a coarse grinding plate into a 5-quart stainless steel bowl.

Add the onions, apricots, salt, pepper, and rosemary to the ground meats. Gently but thoroughly combine the ingredients.

Gently form the veal-pork mixture into four 6-ounce, 1-inch-thick burgers. Cover the burgers with plastic wrap and refrigerate until needed.

Preheat the oven to 375°F.

Heat a well-seasoned flat griddle or large nonstick sauté pan over medium-high heat. When hot, sear the burgers until golden brown, about 2 minutes on each side. Transfer the burgers to a baking sheet with sides and finish cooking in the oven for 10 to 12 minutes.

Toast the rye bread in the oven or in a toaster just prior to removing the burgers from the oven.

Spread the toasted bread slices with Honey Mustard Cream. Serve each Veal and Apricot Burger between 2 slices of the bread, and accompany the burgers with Apple and Walnut Salad.

Honey Mustard Cream

Yields a generous ½ cup

½ cup sour cream
2 tablespoons Dijon mustard
1 tablespoon honey
   Salt and pepper to season

In a small stainless steel bowl, use a rubber spatula to combine the sour cream, mustard, and honey. Adjust the seasoning with salt and pepper, and combine thoroughly. The Honey Mustard Cream can be stored tightly covered in a noncorrosive container in the refrigerator for up to 1 week.

As none of the Scandinavian countries produce grape wines, it would seem natural to suggest a glass of golden beer to accompany this Danish-inspired burger. If you want to become totally immersed in the Scandinavian spirit, try pairing a beer with a very cold shot of Aquavit.

Apple and Walnut Salad

Yields 4 servings

½ cup mayonnaise
¼ teaspoon finely chopped fresh rosemary
   Salt and pepper to season
2 Red Delicious apples, washed
¾ cup diagonally sliced celery
½ cup diced dried apricots
½ cup toasted walnuts

In a 3-quart stainless steel bowl, combine the mayonnaise and rosemary. Adjust the seasoning with salt and pepper, and combine thoroughly.

Core and dice the apples into ½-inch pieces (do not peel). Toss the apples, celery, apricots, and walnuts with the dressing to coat lightly but thoroughly. Serve immediately. The Apple and Walnut Salad will keep tightly covered in the refrigerator for several hours (without the apples discoloring).

This salad was obviously inspired by the traditional Waldorf salad. However, in Vinnie's version, the addition of fresh rosemary and dried apricots gives the recipe a culinarian's innovative touch.

 # Beef Sirloin and Kidney Burger
with Grain-Mustard Butter and Steamed Asparagus

Makes 4 burgers

Charles Palmer
Executive Chef/Owner
Aureole
New York, New York

LEAVE IT TO CHARLES PALMER, WHO HAS NO QUALMS ABOUT TANTALIZING THE TASTE BUDS WITH HIS SPECIAL BRAND OF CUISINE AT THE ELEGANT AUREOLE RESTAURANT, TO DEVISE AN ELEGANT SIRLOIN BURGER THAT GETS A GREAT BIG BOOST OF FLAVOR FROM FRESH BEEF KIDNEYS.

CHARLES' BEEF SIRLOIN AND KIDNEY BURGER REFLECTS HIS POLICY OF RETAINING THE TRUE AND HONEST FLAVOR OF FOOD—YET THROWING IN AN ELEMENT OF SURPRISE.

Charles recommends that a good fragrant dark ale be enjoyed with his burger. He also suggests that his Beef Sirloin and Kidney Burgers would be equally delicious served on sourdough rolls or bread.

1¼ **pounds lean beef sirloin, cut into 1-inch cubes (or 1¼ pounds ground lean beef sirloin)**

½ **pound beef kidneys, trimmed of fat and membrane, and cut into 1-inch cubes (or 6 ounces ground beef kidneys; see Note)**

4 **tablespoons extra-virgin olive oil**

4 **tablespoons finely minced shallots**

½ **teaspoon kosher salt**

½ **teaspoon coarsely ground black pepper**

2 **tablespoons unsalted butter**

2 **large onions (1½ pounds), sliced thin**
   Salt and pepper to season

1 **cup chicken stock**

4 **Onion Rolls (see page 89), cut in half**

If using beef and kidney cubes, grind through a meat grinder fitted with a coarse grinding plate into a 5-quart stainless steel bowl.

Gently but thoroughly combine the ground meats with 3 tablespoons olive oil, shallots, kosher salt, and coarsely ground black pepper.

Gently form the sirloin-kidney mixture into four 6-¾-ounce, 1-inch-thick burgers. Cover the burgers with plastic wrap and refrigerate until needed.

Heat the butter in a large nonstick sauté pan over medium heat. When melted, add the onions, season with salt and pepper, and sauté until caramelized, 25 to 30 minutes. Add the chicken stock and bring to a boil. Lower the heat and simmer very slowly for 15 minutes. The caramelized onions may be kept warm while preparing the remainder of the recipe, or they can be cooled, refrigerated, and reheated when needed.

Prior to grilling, brush the burgers with remaining 1 tablespoon olive oil.

Grill the burgers over a medium wood or charcoal fire. Cook to the desired doneness: 3 to 4 minutes on each side for rare, 5 to 6 minutes on each side for medium, and 8 to 9 minutes on each side for well-done. (This burger may also be cooked on a well-seasoned flat griddle or in a large nonstick sauté pan over medium-high heat. Cook for about the same amount of time as listed for grilling.)

Toast the rolls, cut side down, on the grill or griddle or in a nonstick sauté pan until golden brown, about 1 minute. Spread the toasted rolls with Grain-Mustard Butter. Serve the burgers on the rolls with the warm caramelized onions, accompanied by Steamed Asparagus.

Note: Kidneys can be found, fresh or frozen, in most major supermarkets (Charles recommends using fresh kidneys). A fresh beef kidney will have a clean, although slightly acidic, smell. Avoid purchasing kidneys that have lost their bright red color or that have an aroma that makes you wrinkle your nose.

Grain-Mustard Butter

Yields ¾ cup

4 ounces unsalted butter, softened
2 tablespoons coarse-ground whole-grain prepared mustard (see Note)
½ teaspoon fresh lemon juice
½ teaspoon salt
½ teaspoon freshly ground black pepper

In a small stainless steel bowl, combine the butter and mustard using a rubber spatula, and stir until smooth. Add the lemon juice, salt, and pepper, and stir until the lemon juice is incorporated. The butter can be stored covered in the refrigerator for several days.

Note: The choice of gourmet mustards is practically endless. One that delivers excellent taste is the whole-grain *moutarde de meaux* (Pommery brand).

Steamed Asparagus

Yields 4 servings

2 tablespoons unsalted butter
  Zest of 1 lemon
½ teaspoon cracked black pepper
1½ pounds asparagus
½ teaspoon salt

In a small stainless steel bowl, combine the butter, lemon zest, and pepper. Set aside at room temperature until needed.

Snap the woody end from each stalk of the asparagus. Lightly peel the asparagus and cut each stalk diagonally into 1-inch pieces.

Heat ¼ cup water and the salt in a large nonstick sauté pan over high heat. When the water begins to boil, add the asparagus pieces, and steam until tender and bright green, about 3 to 4 minutes. Remove the pan from the heat and add the lemon butter. Toss lightly to coat the asparagus pieces. Serve immediately.

Wisconsin Camp-Fire Burger

with Beer and Cheese Bread and
Pan-Fried New Potatoes

Makes 4 burgers

Jon Pierre Peavey
Assistant Chef
The Trellis Restaurant
Williamsburg, Virginia

MUCH OF WHAT JON PIERRE PEAVEY KNEW ABOUT COOKING BEFORE COMING TO THE CULINARY INSTITUTE OF AMERICA CAME THE OLD-FASHIONED WAY— HE LEARNED IT FROM HIS FATHER.

JON PIERRE'S DAD WAS A MASTER OF CAMP-FIRE CUISINE—NOT ENTIRELY UNUSUAL FOR ONE WHO HAILS FROM INDIANHEAD COUNTRY, A.K.A. EAU CLAIRE, WISCONSIN. AS A CHILD, JON PIERRE ENJOYED MANY FISHING AND CAMPING TRIPS WITH HIS FAMILY, AND HE HAS FOND MEMORIES OF HIS FATHER'S OUTDOOR PROWESS. MR. PEAVEY ALWAYS SAID HE COULD SURVIVE IN THE WOODS WITH ONLY A HATCHET, A TRAPPER'S BLANKET, AND A POUND OF SALT. THE FACT IS THAT MR. PEAVEY ALSO HAD A SUBSTANTIAL INVENTORY OF CAMPING EQUIPMENT, INCLUDING A RATHER ONEROUS BUT INVALUABLE IRON COOKING SKILLET. BLACK AND SOOTY, THIS PAN WAS FONDLY REFERRED TO AS "WELL SEASONED"; IT WAS ALWAYS CLEANED BY RUBBING IT WITH BACON GREASE, THEN TURNING IT UPSIDE DOWN OVER THE DYING EMBERS OF THE DAY'S CAMP FIRE. JON PIERRE INHERITED THIS PAN UNDER THE CONDITION THAT IT NEVER BE WASHED WITH ANYTHING AS ODIOUS AS SOAP.

JON PIERRE ALSO INHERITED HIS FATHER'S PASSION FOR DELICIOUS FOOD, AND HIS WISCONSIN CAMP-FIRE BURGER WOULD MAKE HIS LATE FATHER PROUD.

2 **pounds fresh ground beef chuck**
1 **bunch scallions, trimmed and sliced thin diagonally**
5 **tablespoons beer**
2 **teaspoons salt**
1 **teaspoon freshly ground black pepper**
12 **ounces mushrooms, stems trimmed, sliced ¹/₈ inch thick**

In a 5-quart stainless steel bowl, gently but thoroughly combine the ground beef, scallions, beer, salt, and pepper.

Gently form the meat mixture into four 8-ounce, 1¹/₄-inch-thick burgers. Cover the burgers with plastic wrap and refrigerate until needed.

Cut four 18- by 12-inch sheets of aluminum foil. Place 3 ounces mushrooms in the middle of each sheet of foil. Place a burger on top of each portion of mushrooms. Bring 2 edges of the foil together, and roll the foil down to the top of the burger. Twist each end to form a handle. Keep the burgers well chilled until a few moments before cooking.

Cook the burgers directly on the coals of a low wood or charcoal fire. Cook to the desired doneness: 5 minutes on each side for rare, 7 minutes on each side for medium, and 9 minutes on each side for well-done.

Remove the foil packages from the fire. Toast four 1-inch-thick slices of Beer and Cheese Bread on a grill over the fire until golden brown, about 1 minute.

Unfold the foil and place the burgers on the toasted Beer and Cheese Bread. Spoon out any remaining mushrooms from the foil and place on top of the burgers. Serve immediately with Pan-Fried New Potatoes.

Beer and Cheese Bread

Makes I loaf (eight I-inch slices)

9   tablespoons unsalted butter
3   cups all-purpose flour
1   cup grated extra-sharp cheddar cheese
    (see Note)
1/2   cup yellow cornmeal
4   teaspoons baking powder
1 1/2   teaspoons salt
1   tablespoon honey
12   ounces beer
2   large eggs, lightly beaten

Preheat the oven to 375°F.

Coat the inside of a 9- by 5-inch loaf pan with 1 table-spoon butter.

In a 5-quart stainless steel bowl, thoroughly combine the flour, cheddar, cornmeal, baking powder, and salt.

Heat the remaining 8 tablespoons butter with the honey in a small saucepan over medium heat. When the butter has melted, add to the dry ingredients. Add the beer and eggs. Use a rubber spatula and stir well to combine.

Pour the batter into the buttered loaf pan and bake for 45 minutes. Remove the bread from the oven and cool for 15 minutes before removing from the pan. Cool for at least 30 minutes before slicing.

Note: Jon Pierre enthusiastically recommends using Cooper brand extra-sharp Wisconsin cheddar for his recipe. This cheese has just the right edge to give the quick bread its distinctive flavor.

Jon Pierre recommends that any Wisconsin camping trip include, in addition to the requisite bottle of Heinz ketchup, several well-chilled bottles of Leinenkugel's beer from Chippewa Falls, Wisconsin.

Pan-Fried New Potatoes

Yields 4 servings

1   tablespoon salt
2   pounds new potatoes or small (1 1/2-inch
    diameter) red bliss potatoes, scrubbed but not
    peeled
4   slices smoked bacon (about 3 ounces), cut into
    1/2-inch pieces
    Salt and freshly ground black pepper to
    season
1 1/2   cups sliced onions

Heat 2 quarts water and 1 tablespoon salt in a 6-quart saucepan over high heat. Bring to a boil. Add the potatoes, reduce the heat to medium-high, and simmer until potatoes are tender, about 20 minutes. Drain the potatoes and cool uncovered in the refrigerator.

Slice the cooled potatoes 1/2 inch thick. Heat a large nonstick sauté pan or a heavy iron skillet over medium-high heat. When the pan is hot, add the bacon and fry until lightly browned, about 3 1/2 to 4 minutes. Push the bacon to the edges of the pan and spread the potatoes onto the bottom of the pan. Season with salt and pepper, and cook undisturbed until browned, about 15 minutes.

Spread the onions over the potatoes. Lightly season with salt and pepper, and combine the onions, potatoes, and bacon. Cook for an additional 10 to 15 minutes, stirring every 3 to 4 minutes. Remove from the heat and serve immediately.

The Pan-Fried New Potatoes may be kept warm in a 200°F oven for up to 30 minutes before serving.

Although the cooking may be easier in a nonstick sauté pan, the iron skillet easily conjures up camp-fire imagery. Don't worry, though; the potatoes will be appreciated no matter what cooking pan you use.

Westmoreland Bistro Burger

with Yukon Gold Potato Salad

Makes 4 burgers

John and Caprial Pence

Chefs/Owners
Westmoreland Bistro and Wines
Portland, Oregon

THE RELATIONSHIP BETWEEN JOHN AND CAPRIAL PENCE, BOTH GRADUATES OF THE CULINARY INSTITUTE OF AMERICA, CAN BE DESCRIBED AS NOTHING LESS THAN REMARKABLE. AFTER MOVING TO SEATTLE IMMEDIATELY FOLLOWING GRADUATION, THIS HUSBAND-AND-WIFE TEAM WORKED AT FULLERS RESTAURANT. JOHN EVENTUALLY LEFT TO BECOME THE CHEF AT LA FLEUR AND THEN AT PLACE PIGALLE.

AFTER CAPRIAL GAVE BIRTH TO THEIR SON, JOHN STAYED HOME AND DEVOTED HIS TIME AND ENERGY TO RAISING THE CHILD. MEANWHILE, CAPRIAL BECAME THE CHEF AT FULLERS, GAINING MUCH NATIONAL AND INTERNATIONAL PRESS. EVENTUALLY, JOHN RETURNED TO FULLERS AS CO-CHEF WITH CAPRIAL.

IN 1992, THEIR LONG-HELD DREAM CAME TRUE: THEY PURCHASED WESTMORELAND BISTRO AND WINES, A TWENTY-THREE-SEAT RESTAURANT AND RETAIL WINE STORE IN PORTLAND, OREGON.

JOHN AND CAPRIAL HOPE YOU WILL VISIT WHEN IN PORTLAND AND SAVOR A WESTMORELAND BISTRO BURGER AT THE SOURCE.

6 medium shallots, peeled
4 cloves garlic, peeled
2 tablespoons extra-virgin olive oil
1 tablespoon balsamic vinegar
1 teaspoon salt
1/2 teaspoon green peppercorns
1/2 teaspoon chopped fresh tarragon
1 1/2 pounds ground beef chuck
1 18-inch loaf French bread, cut in half lengthwise
4 thin slices cooked pancetta (see Note)
2 ounces fresh goat cheese, divided into 4 equal parts

Preheat the oven to 350°F.

Place the shallots and garlic in a pie tin. Sprinkle with the olive oil and balsamic vinegar, and season with the salt, peppercorns, and tarragon. Cover the pie tin with aluminum foil. Place in the oven, and roast the shallots and garlic until tender, about 35 minutes.

Place the roasted shallot-garlic mixture in the bowl of a food processor fitted with a metal blade, and pulse until roughly pureed, about 10 seconds. Transfer to a dinner plate and place uncovered in the refrigerator to cool.

In a 5-quart stainless steel bowl, gently but thoroughly combine the ground beef with the cooled shallot-garlic mixture.

Gently form the ground beef mixture into four 6-ounce, 1 1/4-inch-thick, oval-shaped burgers. Cover the burgers with plastic wrap and refrigerate until needed.

Grill the burgers over a medium wood or charcoal fire. Cook to the desired doneness: about 3 to 4 minutes on each side for rare, 6 to 7 minutes on each side for medium, and 8 to 9 minutes on each side for well-done. (This burger may also be cooked on a well-seasoned flat griddle or in a large nonstick sauté pan over medium-high heat. Cook for about the same amout of time as listed for grilling.)

While the burgers are cooking, toast the French bread on the grill or griddle or in a nonstick sauté pan, cut side down, until golden brown, about 1 minute. Cut the French bread halves into 4-inch-long portions. Warm the cooked pancetta slices over the fire or in a nonstick sauté pan for a few moments. Place each cooked burger on a bottom portion of the grilled bread and top each with a portion of the goat cheese, 1 slice of the pancetta, and the top portion of the grilled French bread. Serve immediately, accompanied by Yukon Gold Potato Salad.

Note: Pancetta is an Italian bacon that is rolled into a solid round; it resembles salt pork more than bacon. Look for pancetta in gourmet markets.

Yukon Gold Potato Salad

Yields 4 servings

2   **shallots, trimmed and cut in half lengthwise**
1/4 **cup plus 1 tablespoon extra-virgin olive oil**
2   **pounds small (about 2 1/2-inch diameter) unpeeled Yukon gold potatoes**
    Juice of 1 lemon
1   **tablespoon cider vinegar**
1   **teaspoon chopped fresh thyme**
1   **teaspoon salt**
1/2 **teaspoon cracked black pepper**

Preheat the oven to 325°F.

Place the shallots, cut side down, in the bottom of a glass baking dish or pie tin, and drizzle them with 1 tablespoon olive oil. Cover the shallots with aluminum foil and roast in the oven until tender and golden brown, about 25 minutes. Remove the shallots from the oven and allow them to cool, uncovered, in the olive oil at room temperature.

Place the potatoes in a 6-quart pot and cover with cold water. Bring to a boil over high heat, then adjust the heat and simmer slowly until potatoes are cooked through, about 35 to 40 minutes. Drain the water from the potatoes, then transfer to a large plate and cool, uncovered, in the refrigerator for at least 1 hour.

In a 3-quart stainless steel bowl, whisk together the remaining 1/4 cup olive oil, lemon juice, cider vinegar, thyme, salt, and pepper. Combine thoroughly.

Peel the skins from the cooled shallots and thinly slice them lengthwise.

Cut the cooled potatoes into quarters lengthwise, then cut the quarters into 1/2-inch-thick slices.

Use a rubber spatula to gently but thoroughly combine the roasted shallots and sliced potatoes with the dressing. Serve immediately or store tightly covered in a noncorrosive container for up to 3 days.

Fingerling potatoes are also particularly good in this recipe.

Vietnamese Sirloin Burger
with Cucumber and Carrot Salad

Makes 6 burgers

Nicole Routhier
Cookbook Author
New York, New York

IF WRITING AN AWARD-WINNING COOKBOOK WAS NOT FOREMOST ON NICOLE ROUTHIER'S MIND WHEN SHE WAS A STUDENT AT THE CULINARY INSTITUTE OF AMERICA, IT IS NOW CERTAINLY AT THE TOP OF HER LIST OF ACHIEVEMENTS. NICOLE IS THE AUTHOR OF THE CRITICALLY ACCLAIMED *FOODS OF VIETNAM*. HER MOST RECENT BOOK, *COOKING UNDER WRAPS*, IS SURE TO PUT HER IN THE BIG LEAGUE OF BEST-SELLING AUTHORS.

NICOLE'S VIETNAMESE SIRLOIN BURGER IS A NATURAL OUTCOME OF HER BIRTHPLACE, TASTES, AND INTERESTS. HAMBURGERS ARE ONE OF HER FAVORITE FOODS, AND SHE CONSIDERS THEM ONE OF THE MOST FLAVORFUL AND SATISFYING MEALS. HER RECIPE IS AN ADAPTATION OF A POPULAR VIETNAMESE SPECIALTY.

> *This burger darkens very quickly if cooked over a fire that is too hot. The sugar in the fish sauce mixture makes the meat caramelize rapidly over a hot fire, so keep an eye on the flame. It is better to err in favor of a fire that is too low, which will increase cooking times, rather than a hot fire, which will render the burgers inedible.*

1/3 cup granulated sugar
2 tablespoons fish sauce (see Note on following page)
2 tablespoons light soy sauce
2 tablespoons warm water
1 cup minced onions
4 teaspoons minced garlic
1/4 teaspoon freshly ground black pepper
2 pounds ground beef sirloin
6 Onion Rolls (see page 89), cut in half
4 Boston lettuce leaves, washed and dried
4 slices ripe red tomatoes

Heat the sugar in a medium nonstick sauté pan over medium-high heat, swirling the pan until the sugar has thoroughly melted and is lightly browned, about 2 1/2 minutes. Remove from the heat and stir in the fish sauce, soy sauce, and warm water, being careful to avoid splattering. Return the pan to medium heat and stir the mixture constantly until completely liquefied, about 3 to 4 minutes. Add the onions, garlic, and pepper, stirring to combine. Transfer the mixture to a 5-quart stainless steel bowl and cool in the refrigerator until ready to use.

Gently but thoroughly combine the ground beef with the cooled fish sauce mixture. Cover with plastic wrap and allow to stand at room temperature for 15 minutes (so that the flavors may commingle).

Gently form the ground beef mixture into six 6-ounce, 1-inch-thick burgers. Cover with plastic wrap and refrigerate until needed.

Grill the burgers over a low wood or charcoal fire. Cook to the desired doneness: about 3 to 4 minutes on each side for rare, 5 to 6 minutes on each side for medium, and 8 to 9 minutes on each side for well-done. (This burger may also be cooked on a well-seasoned flat griddle or in a large nonstick sauté pan over medium heat. Cook for about the same amount of time as listed for grilling.)

Toast the rolls, cut side down, on the grill or griddle or in a nonstick sauté pan until golden brown, about 1 minute. Place each burger on the bottom half of a roll, and top with 1 of the lettuce leaves, 1 of the tomato slices, and the other half of the roll. Serve immediately accompanied by Cucumber and Carrot Salad.

Nicole says that in Vietnam, savory-sweet burgers shaped into tiny patties are served accompanied by fresh lettuce leaves, soft noodles, pickles, and lots of fresh herbs. In her recipe, Nicole has transformed the patties into a single burger and served them with Cucumber and Carrot Salad on the side.

Note: Not for the faint of nose, fish sauces pack an astonishingly odoriferous wallop. This limpid sauce takes some getting used to, but it will almost certainly lend a heady and pleasant flavor when used judiciously. Ask your Asian grocer for recommended brands.

Cucumber and Carrot Salad

Yields 6 servings

1/2	cup unseasoned rice vinegar or distilled white vinegar
2	tablespoons granulated sugar
1/2	teaspoon salt
1/2	cup cold water
1	tablespoon fish sauce
1/2	teaspoon dried red pepper flakes
2	medium cucumbers, peeled, cut in half, seeded, and sliced thin diagonally
2	medium carrots, peeled and sliced thin diagonally
1	small red onion, sliced thin and rinsed well in cold water
2	tablespoons chopped fresh cilantro

Heat the rice vinegar or white vinegar, sugar, and salt in a 1-quart saucepan over medium-high heat. Bring to a boil, and stir to dissolve the sugar. Transfer the mixture to a 3-quart stainless steel bowl. Stir in the cold water, fish sauce, and red pepper flakes. Stir to combine. Allow the mixture to cool to room temperature. Add the vegetables and cilantro, and gently toss to combine. Refrigerate and allow the mixture to marinate for at least 30 minutes before serving.

This salad will keep covered in the refrigerator for 2 to 3 days. Drain any excess liquid before serving.

Classic Grilled Hamburger
with Summer Vegetable Salad

Makes 4 burgers

L. Timothy Ryan
Vice President of Education
The Culinary Institute of America
Hyde Park, New York

AFTER FIVE YEARS OF INDUSTRY EXPERIENCE FOLLOWING HIS GRADUATION FROM THE INSTITUTE, TIM RETURNED TO HYDE PARK IN 1982 AS A MEMBER OF THE PROJECT TEAM THAT DEVELOPED THE AMERICAN BOUNTY RESTAURANT DURING HIS TIME AS CHEF-INSTRUCTOR AT THE AMERICAN BOUNTY, TIM WAS SELECTED FOR THE 1983 *FOOD & WINE* MAGAZINE HONOR ROLL OF AMERICAN CHEFS. SINCE THEN, TIM, NOW RESPONSIBLE FOR DIRECTING AND COORDINATING THE INSTITUTE'S EDUCATIONAL PROGRAMS, HAS SEEMINGLY WON ENOUGH GOLD IN NATIONAL AND INTERNATIONAL CULINARY COMPETITION TO SOLVE THE NATIONAL DEFICIT CRISIS.

TIM RYAN HAS THE DISTINCTION OF BEING THE YOUNGEST CHEF IN THE UNITED STATES TO RECEIVE MASTER CHEF CERTIFICATION FROM THE AMERICAN CULINARY FEDERATION. IN 1985, HE WAS NAMED A RECIPIENT OF THE MEDAL OF CULINARY EXCELLENCE FROM THE FRENCH REPUBLIC, CONSIDERED THE HIGHEST RECOGNITION OF CULINARY ACHIEVEMENT.

IT IS NO SURPRISE THAT AN AMERICAN OF SUCH IMPECCABLE CULINARY CREDENTIALS OFFERS THE QUINTESSENTIAL BURGER RECIPE.

2 **pounds ground beef chuck**
2 **tablespoons cold water**
Salt and freshly ground black pepper to season
4 **Best Burger Buns (see page 109), cut in half**

4 **iceberg lettuce leaves, washed and dried**
4 **slices ripe red tomatoes**
Ketchup

In a 5-quart stainless steel bowl, gently but thoroughly combine the ground beef and cold water.

Gently form the beef into four 8-ounce, 1¼-inch-thick burgers. Cover the burgers with plastic wrap and refrigerate until needed.

Prior to grilling, generously season the burgers with salt and pepper.

Grill the burgers over a medium wood or charcoal fire. Cook to the desired doneness: about 4 to 5 minutes on each side for rare, 6 to 7 minutes on each side for medium, and 8 to 9 minutes on each side for well-done. (This burger may also be cooked on a well-seasoned flat griddle or in a large nonstick sauté pan over medium-high heat. Cook for about the same amount of time as listed for grilling.)

Remove the burgers from the grill. Toast the buns, cut side down, on the grill or griddle or in a nonstick sauté pan until golden brown, about 1 minute.

Serve the burgers on the toasted buns with the lettuce, tomatoes, and ketchup and accompanied by Summer Vegetable Salad.

> *Tim suggests that you serve his Classic Grilled Hamburger with two other natural accompaniments: french fries, of course, and a very cold, strikingly refreshing glass of Coke.*

Summary Vegetable Salad

Yields 4 servings

¾ cup extra-virgin olive oil
2 tablespoons balsamic vinegar
   Salt and pepper to season
2 cloves garlic, peeled
½ cup fresh lemon juice
2 large artichokes
½ pound tiny green beans (*haricots vert*), trimmed
4 plum tomatoes, peeled, seeded, and chopped
1 large red bell pepper, roasted, skinned, seeded, and cut into long, thin strips
1 small red onion, sliced thin
½ head frisée, cut into 2-inch pieces, washed, and dried (see Note)
4 ounces fresh buffalo milk mozzarella cheese, diced (see Note)
½ bunch Italian parsley leaves, washed and dried
3 large basil leaves, washed, dried, and cut into thin strips
1 bunch chives, sliced thin

In a stainless steel bowl, whisk together the olive oil and balsamic vinegar. Adjust the seasoning with salt and pepper, and combine thoroughly. Add the garlic, and allow to marinate at room temperature for at least 30 minutes. Discard the garlic cloves before dressing the salad.

In a 6-quart stainless steel or glass saucepan, bring to a boil 3 quarts lightly salted water with ¼ cup lemon juice (this will be the cooking water). While the water is heating, remove the outer leaves from the artichokes. Slice off the flower about one-third of the way down from the top. Using a sharp-edged spoon, scrape out the thistle from the center of the cut artichokes. Trim each stem to about ¼ inch. Place the artichokes, as soon as both have been

cut and trimmed, into 6 cups water acidulated with the remaining ¼ cup lemon juice. Keep the artichokes in this acidulated water until the cooking water begins to boil (do not hold the artichokes in the acidulated water for a prolonged period of time, or they will acquire a sour taste). Cook the artichokes in the boiling water until cooked through, about 12 minutes. Drain the cooked artichokes, then plunge into ice water. When cool, peel the fibrous outer layer from the artichokes and slice lengthwise into ¼-inch-thick pieces.

Cook the green beans in 2 quarts lightly salted boiling water until tender, about 4 to 5 minutes. Drain the beans, then immediately plunge into ice water to stop the cooking and keep the beans bright green. Remove from the ice water and drain well.

In a 5-quart stainless steel bowl, combine the cooked artichokes, green beans, plum tomatoes, red bell peppers, red onions, frisée, mozzarella, parsley, and basil. Toss together with the dressing, sprinkle the chives on top of the salad, and serve immediately.

Note: Frisée is a delicate green with curly, frilly-edged leaves. Look for it in specialty produce markets. You may substitute other chicories such as the more commonly available curly endive.

If you are unable to purchase fresh buffalo milk mozzarella, then substitute a domestically produced fresh mozzarella.

To make the salad in advance (from a few hours to a day), prepare as described above, but do not toss the ingredients with the dressing until a few minutes before serving (otherwise, the green beans will discolor).

California Burger
with Best Parmesan Burger Buns

Makes 4 burgers

Charles Saunders
Executive Chef/Owner
East Side Oyster Bar & Grill
Sonoma, California

WHEN CHARLES SAUNDERS STUDIED POLITICAL SCIENCE AT AMERICAN UNIVERSITY IN WASHINGTON, D.C., HE FOCUSED ON INTERNATIONAL STUDIES AND FOREIGN LANGUAGES. BUT HIS SPARE TIME WAS FILLED WITH MANY HOURS OF GASTRONOMIC PEREGRINATIONS. SO IT IS NOT SURPRISING THAT SEVERAL YEARS LATER, CHARLES' EAGERNESS TO EXPAND HIS CULINARY INTERESTS BROUGHT HIM TO THE CULINARY INSTITUTE. FOLLOWING HIS GRADUATION, CHARLES' TWO WORLDS MERGED WHEN HE SERVED AS CHEF AT THE U.S. EMBASSY IN BERN, SWITZERLAND, FROM 1981 TO 1983, BECOMING THE FIRST AMERICAN CHEF AT AN AMERICAN EMBASSY IN EUROPE TO COOK AT THE PRIVATE RESIDENCE OF AN AMBASSADOR.

NOW ENSCONCED AT HIS OWN RESTAURANT, CHARLES HAS CONCENTRATED ON THE CUISINE OF CALIFORNIA FOR HIS BURGER RECIPE.

To add a spicy twist to the California Burgers, season the mayonnaise with some lemon juice, salt, freshly ground pepper, and a pinch each of cayenne pepper, chili powder, and cumin.

3/4 pound lean ground beef chuck
3/4 pound lean ground beef sirloin
Salt and freshly ground black pepper to season
2 ripe avocados
4 1/4-inch-thick slices red onions
4 tablespoons mayonnaise
4 Bibb lettuce leaves, washed and dried
4 1/4-inch-thick slices ripe tomatoes

In a 5-quart stainless steel bowl, gently combine the ground beef chuck and ground beef sirloin.

Gently form the beef into four 6-ounce, 1-inch-thick burgers. Season each with salt and pepper. Cover the burgers with plastic wrap and refrigerate until needed.

Cut, pit, and peel the avocados. Thinly slice (about 1/8 inch thick) the avocado halves from end to end. (The preparation of the avocados should be done just a few minutes before grilling the burgers; otherwise, the avocados will oxidize and discolor.)

Grill the burgers over a medium wood or charcoal fire. Cook to the desired doneness: 3 to 4 minutes on each side for rare, 5 to 6 minutes on each side for medium, and 8 to 9 minutes on each side for well-done. (This burger may also be cooked on a well-seasoned flat griddle or in a large nonstick sauté pan over medium-high heat. Cook for about the same amount of time as listed for grilling.)

While the burgers are being grilled, also grill the red onions. Place the onion slices on a well-oiled area of the grill, and season with salt and pepper. Cook for 3 to 4 minutes on each side. (The onions could also be cooked in a nonstick sauté pan.)

Remove the burgers and the onion slices from the grill. Cut 4 Best Parmesan Burger Buns in half. Toast the buns, cut side down, on the grill or griddle or in a nonstick sauté pan until golden brown, about 1 minute. Spread 1/2 tablespoon mayonnaise onto each bun half. Place each burger on the bottom half of a bun and top with 1 of the lettuce leaves, 1 of the tomato slices, avocado slices, 1 of the grilled onion slices, and a top bun half. Serve the burgers immediately.

The Best Burger Buns and The Best Parmesan Burger Buns

Makes 12 buns

½ teaspoon granulated sugar
½ cup plus 2 tablespoons warm water
1 teaspoon active dry yeast
4¼ cups all-purpose flour
½ cup milk
1 large egg, at room temperature
2 tablespoons plus 1 teaspoon olive oil
1 teaspoon salt
¼ cup yellow cornmeal
1 large egg white

1 cup freshly grated Parmesan cheese (for the Parmesan Burger Buns)

In the bowl of an electric mixer, dissolve the sugar in the warm water. Add the yeast and stir gently to dissolve. Allow the mixture to stand and foam for 6 to 8 minutes.

Place the mixing bowl on an electric mixer fitted with a dough hook. On top of the yeast mixture, add 4 cups flour (also add the Parmesan if making The Best Parmesan Burger Buns) and the milk, egg, 2 tablespoons olive oil, and salt. Mix on low speed for 1 minute, then scrape down the sides of the bowl. Continue to mix on low until the dough forms a ball, about 4 to 5 minutes. If the dough attaches itself to the dough hook at any time, stop the mixer and pull the dough off the hook. (If a table-model electric mixer is not available, follow the directions using a hand-held mixer or kneading by hand. The mixing times will increase depending upon which alternative method is used.)

Knead the dough for 5 to 6 minutes on a clean, dry, lightly floured work surface, using the remaining ¼ cup flour as necessary.

Coat the inside of a stainless steel bowl with the remaining 1 teaspoon olive oil. Place the dough in the bowl and wipe the bowl with the dough. Cover the bowl with a damp towel. Allow the dough to rise in a warm location until the dough has doubled in volume, about 2 hours.

Preheat the oven to 425°F.

Place the dough on a lightly floured work surface. Punch down the dough. Use a sharp knife to cut the dough into 12 equal portions. Shape each dough portion into a ball. Flatten each dough ball to ½ inch thick. Place the flattened dough balls on a 15- by 10-inch baking sheet that has been sprinkled with the cornmeal. Cover the dough with a damp towel and allow to rise in a warm location until doubled in size, about 45 minutes.

Whisk the egg white, then lightly brush over the flattened dough balls. Use a sharp knife or a razor blade to cut an X into the top of each dough ball, then bake for 12 to 14 minutes.

Allow the buns to cool thoroughly before slicing them horizontally.

The thoroughly cooled buns may be frozen for several weeks in resealable plastic bags. Thaw the buns before grilling or toasting in the oven.

> *In the vernacular of the "Left Coast" (Charles' sobriquet for the West Coast), this bun is indeed quite awesome, especially if prepared with the Parmesan cheese, which is what Charles would have you do.*

> *Charles recommends that a large cloth napkin be supplied for each burger eater. And as long as he is making recommendations, Charles also suggests you enjoy a young Pinot Noir with the California Burger, specifically one of those brashly fresh and fruity wines that comes from Sonoma wine country.*

West Indies Burger
with Mango Chutney and Fried Plantains

Makes 4 burgers

Chris Schlesinger
Chef/Owner
East Coast Grill
Cambridge, Massachusetts

ANYONE WHO HAS EATEN CHRIS
SCHLESINGER'S EXCITING FOOD WILL NOT
NEED TO PONDER THE ORIGINS OF HIS
WEST INDIES BURGER. MANY OF CHRIS'
CULINARY INSPIRATIONS DERIVE FROM THE
TIME HE "LABORED" OVER HOT STOVES
IN THE CARIBBEAN FOLLOWING HIS
GRADUATION FROM THE CULINARY
INSTITUTE OF AMERICA.

SINCE OPENING THE EAST COAST GRILL
IN 1985, CHRIS HAS FIRED THE CULINARY
LANDSCAPE WITH HIS EXPLOSIVE FLAVORS.
HIS BEST-SELLING COOKBOOK *THE THRILL
OF THE GRILL* IS A TRIBUTE TO HIS
INCENDIARY CUISINE.

> *Chris insists that the only beverage
> allowable with his burger is a very
> cold 16-ounce can of Budweiser.*

1½	**pounds lean ground beef chuck**
3	**tablespoons chopped fresh cilantro**
1	**tablespoon minced garlic**
2	**teaspoons fresh lime juice**
1	**teaspoon curry powder**
1	**teaspoon ground cumin**
1	**teaspoon ground allspice**
3	**to 5 dashes Tabasco Sauce**
	Salt and freshly cracked black pepper to season
4	**Best Burger Buns (see page 109), cut in half, or other favorite bread**

In a 5-quart stainless steel bowl, gently but thoroughly combine the
ground beef with the cilantro, garlic, lime juice, curry powder, cumin, allspice,
Tabasco Sauce, and salt and pepper to season.

Gently form the seasoned beef into four 6-ounce, ¾-inch-thick burgers.
Cover the burgers with plastic wrap and refrigerate until needed.

Grill the burgers over a medium wood or charcoal fire. Cook to the desired
doneness: 3 to 4 minutes on each side for rare, 5 to 6 minutes on each side for
medium, and 8 to 9 minutes on each side for well-done. (This burger may
also be cooked on a well-seasoned flat griddle or in a nonstick sauté pan
over medium-high heat. Cook for about the same amount of time as listed
for grilling.)

Remove the burgers from the grill. Toast the buns, cut side down, on the
grill or griddle or in a nonstick sauté pan until golden brown, about 1 minute.
Place each burger on the bottom half of a bun and top with Mango Chutney.
Cover the chutney with the top half of the bun, and serve with Fried Plantains.

Mango Chutney

Yields 1 quart

2 tablespoons vegetable oil
2 large onions, diced
3 ripe mangoes, peeled, pitted, and cut into large chunks
4 tablespoons tightly packed light brown sugar
4 tablespoons granulated sugar
1/4 cup raisins
1 tablespoon molasses
1 teaspoon salt
1/2 teaspoon freshly cracked white pepper
1/4 teaspoon ground allspice
1/2 cup white vinegar
2 tablespoons fresh lemon juice

Heat the vegetable oil in a 5-quart stainless steel saucepan over medium heat. When hot, add the onions. Sauté until the onions are translucent, about 6 to 8 minutes.

Add the mango chunks, stir, and cook for 4 minutes.

Add the remaining ingredients except 1/4 cup white vinegar and the lemon juice. Reduce the heat to low and simmer uncovered for 1 hour, stirring frequently to prevent the mixture from burning (if necessary, add a tablespoon or two of water during the simmering to prevent the sticking and burning of the mixture).

Remove the mixture from the heat. Add the remaining 1/4 cup white vinegar and the lemon juice, and combine thoroughly. Cool the chutney in an ice-water bath until cold. Refrigerate the chutney in a stainless steel or other noncorrosive container. Keep refrigerated for 12 hours before serving. The chutney will keep tightly covered in the refrigerator for up to 6 weeks.

> *Chris Schlesinger recommends that the chutney be served at room temperature to optimize its flavor.*

Fried Plantains

Yields 4 servings

2 green plantains (see Note)
4 cups vegetable oil
Salt and freshly cracked black pepper to season

Peel the plantains. Cut each plantain into 4 approximately 2-inch-long pieces.

Heat the vegetable oil in a deep fryer (or high-sided, heavy-duty pot) to a temperature of 350°F.

Drop the plantain pieces into the hot oil, 2 at a time, and cook them until well browned, about 2 to 3 minutes. Remove them from the oil and drain on paper towels.

Stand each fried section upright on a table, and with a heavy frying pan, mash each round as flat as a pancake using steady pressure rather than sharp blows.

Put the mashed sections back into the hot oil, 2 at a time, and cook until the entire surface is golden brown, about 2 minutes.

Remove, drain, and season the fried plantains liberally with salt and pepper.

Note: Sometimes known as cooking bananas, plantains can usually be found in grocery stores near Latin-American neighborhoods. The plantain's rapidly expanding popularity has also created demand at most well-stocked grocery stores and produce markets.

Although the hard and starchy texture of a green plantain yields the most favorable results for this recipe, it is also feasible to use riper plantains. The peel of a more mature plantain will range from brown to black. Do not be put off by a lack of aesthetics; riper plantains yield a creamy and sweet fruit.

> *These fried plantains were fondly nicknamed "tropical french fries" in* The Thrill of the Grill.

Shrimp Boulette Po' Boy Burger
with Homemade Worcestershire Sauce
and Creole Sauce

Makes 4 burgers

Jamie Shannon
Executive Chef
Commander's Palace
New Orleans, Louisiana

JAMIE SHANNON'S CULINARY EXPERIENCE BEGAN DURING HIS BOYHOOD ON THE NEW JERSEY SHORE. HE SPENT MANY SUMMER DAYS THERE AT HIS GRANDPARENTS' FARM, FEASTING ON GREAT HOMEMADE DISHES PREPARED FROM INGREDIENTS FRESH FROM THE LAND. FOODS THAT DID NOT COME FROM THE FARM CAME FROM SICILIAN FISHERMEN, FROM CRAB TRAPS JAMIE SET IN THE "BACKYARD," AND FROM STREET VENDORS, WHO SOLD FRESH PASTA AND CHEESES.

AFTER LEARNING THE BASIC COOKING TECHNIQUES WHILE WORKING IN A LOCAL CAFETERIA, JAMIE POLISHED HIS SKILLS IN RESTAURANTS IN THE RESORT TOWN OF WILDWOOD, NEW JERSEY, AND THEN ENROLLED AT THE CULINARY INSTITUTE OF AMERICA. THERE HE DECIDED TO PURSUE REGIONAL AMERICAN COOKING AS HIS SPECIALTY, AND FOLLOWING GRADUATION, HE CHOSE NEW ORLEANS AS HIS HOME BASE. JAMIE JOINED COMMANDER'S PALACE IN 1984 AS A SAUCIER, WORKED HIS WAY THROUGH THE KITCHEN BRIGADE, AND EVENTUALLY BECAME EXECUTIVE CHEF OF THIS INTERNATIONALLY ACCLAIMED RESTAURANT.

Enjoy this zesty burger with a cold beer or experiment with a vivaciously fruity and spicy Gewürztraminer.

1	teaspoon peanut oil
1/2	cup minced onions
2	teaspoons minced garlic
1/2	cup finely diced celery
1/4	cup finely diced red bell peppers
1/4	cup finely diced green bell peppers
1/4	cup finely diced yellow bell peppers
1	small jalapeño chile, roasted, skinned, seeded, and minced
1 1/2	pounds medium shrimp, peeled and deveined
2	tablespoons chopped fresh chives
2	tablespoons chopped fresh parsley
1	tablespoon chopped fresh basil
1	tablespoon chopped fresh thyme
	Salt and white pepper to season
1	18-inch loaf French bread

Heat the peanut oil in a large nonstick sauté pan over medium-high heat. When hot, add the onions and garlic, and sauté until the onions are translucent, about 2 to 3 minutes. Add the celery, red bell peppers, green bell peppers, yellow bell peppers, and no more than 1 teaspoon minced jalapeño, and continue to sauté for 5 minutes. Transfer the mixture to a dinner plate and place uncovered in the refrigerator to cool.

Grind shrimp through a meat grinder fitted with a coarse grinding plate into a 5-quart stainless steel bowl. Gently but thoroughly combine the ground shrimp with the cooled vegetable mixture, chives, parsley, basil, and thyme. Season with salt and pepper.

Gently form the mixture into eight 3 1/2-ounce, 3/4-inch-thick burgers. Cover the burgers and refrigerate until needed.

Preheat the oven to 225°F.

Trim 1 inch from each end of the loaf of French bread. Cut the trimmed loaf into four 4-inch-long portions. Cut each portion in half. Crisp the bread in the oven while cooking the burgers.

Grill the shrimp burgers over a medium-high wood or charcoal fire, 5 to 6 minutes on each side, basting with about 1 teaspoon Homemade Worcestershire Sauce per burger. Serve 2 of the shrimp burgers on each portion of the crusty French bread, topped with Creole Sauce.

Homemade Worcestershire Sauce

Yields 1½ cups

2   teaspoons olive oil
1½ cups diced onions
3   tablespoons grated fresh horseradish root
1   jalapeño chile, seeded and chopped
3   teaspoons minced garlic
2   cups distilled white vinegar
1   cup dark corn syrup
½   cup molasses
½   cup water
1   lemon, peeled and chopped
1   anchovy fillet
6   whole cloves
2   teaspoons salt
½   teaspoon cracked black pepper

Heat the olive oil in a 4-quart saucepan over medium-high heat. When hot, add the onions, horseradish, jalapeños, and garlic, and cook for 3 to 4 minutes, stirring frequently. Add the remaining ingredients and stir to combine. Bring the mixture to a boil. Reduce the heat and simmer until slightly thickened, about 2½ to 3 hours.

Strain through a fine-mesh strainer or cheesecloth, then cool in an ice-water bath and store tightly covered in the refrigerator.

Although Jamie stores his Homemade Worcestershire Sauce in wooden vats, the sauce can be kept tightly covered in a noncorrosive container in the refrigerator for up to several weeks.

> *This Homemade Worcestershire Sauce has as many uses as you might imagine. Since the yield for this recipe is more than will be necessary to baste 4 Shrimp Boulette Po' Boy Burgers, you will probably find yourself basting chicken, chops, and fish with this wonderful concoction.*

Creole Sauce

Yields 2¾ cups

2   teaspoons extra-virgin olive oil
1   teaspoon paprika
1   small onion, peeled and sliced thin
½   cup diced celery
¼   cup diced green peppers
¼   cup diced red peppers
¼   cup diced yellow peppers
1   teaspoon minced garlic
1   small jalapeño chile, roasted, skinned, seeded, and minced
2   teaspoons granulated sugar
¼   cup chicken stock
¼   cup tomato juice
2   teaspoons balsamic vinegar
3   plum tomatoes, peeled, seeded, and chopped
1   tablespoon chopped fresh parsley
1   teaspoon chopped fresh basil
1   teaspoon chopped fresh thyme
    Salt to season

Heat the olive oil in a 3-quart saucepan over medium heat. When hot, add the paprika and cook for 1 minute, stirring constantly to avoid scorching. Add the onions and sauté for 2 to 3 minutes. Then add the celery, green peppers, red peppers, yellow peppers, garlic, and jalapeños, and continue to sauté for an additional 3 to 4 minutes. Add the sugar and stir to dissolve. Add the chicken stock, tomato juice, and balsamic vinegar, and stir to combine. Add the plum tomatoes, parsley, basil, and thyme, and stir gently to combine. Allow the sauce to simmer for 4 to 5 minutes. Adjust the seasoning with salt. Serve immediately, or hold warm in a double boiler for up to 1 hour before using.

The sauce may be cooled in an ice-water bath, then covered and refrigerated for up to 3 days before using. Heat the sauce to a simmer before serving.

"Trini" Burger
with Tropical Fruit Salad

Makes 4 burgers

Arnym Solomon
Vice President of Chain Accounts
CPC Foodservice
Franklin Park, Illinois

SCION OF A PROMINENT TRINIDADIAN
FOOD-SERVICE FAMILY, ARNYM SOLOMON
CARRIES ON THE TRADITION HIS FATHER
SET FORTH FOR THE SOLOMON CLAN.
ARNYM'S DAD, CARL, IS WELL KNOWN
THROUGHOUT THE CARIBBEAN AS AN
EXECUTIVE CHEF AS WELL AS ONE OF THE
FOUNDERS OF TRINIDAD'S IMPORTANT
CULINARY TRAINING FACILITY, THE JOHN
S. DONALDSON TECHNICAL INSTITUTE.
ARNYM HAS SERVED IN FOOD AND
BEVERAGE POSITIONS THROUGHOUT THE
WORLD, INCLUDING THE HUNTINGTON
HILTON IN DALLAS, THE WALDORF-ASTORIA
HOTEL IN NEW YORK CITY, THE TRINIDAD
HILTON IN PORT OF SPAIN, TRINIDAD, AND
HIS ALMA MATER, THE CULINARY
INSTITUTE OF AMERICA.

THE PLACE OF ORIGIN FOR STEEL BANDS
AND CALYPSO, TRINIDAD IS EXCITING,
VIBRANT, AND COLORFUL. LIKEWISE IS
ARNYM SOLOMON'S BURGER RECIPE.

2 **pounds lean ground beef**
4 **tablespoons Worcestershire sauce**
1 **tablespoon chopped fresh thyme**
1 **teaspoon ground cumin**
1 **teaspoon cayenne pepper**
3/4 **cup minced onions**
1 **ounce cheddar cheese, finely diced**

Salt and white pepper to season
4 **Best Burger Buns (see page 109), cut in half**
4 **tablespoons mayonnaise**
4 **large Bibb lettuce leaves, washed and dried**
8 **thin slices ripe tomatoes**
1/2 **medium papaya, peeled, seeded, and sliced thin**

In a 5-quart stainless steel bowl, gently but thoroughly combine the ground beef with the Worcestershire sauce, thyme, cumin, and cayenne pepper.

Gently form the ground beef mixture into eight 4-ounce, 1/4-inch-thick patties.

Use a metal spoon to make a small, shallow indentation in the center of 4 of the beef patties. Combine the onions and cheddar. Divide this mixture into 4 equal portions and place a portion in each indentation. Top with another patty and gently form into a burger, making sure to seal all open edges. Season the burgers with salt and white pepper. Cover the burgers with plastic wrap and refrigerate until needed.

Grill the burgers over a medium wood or charcoal fire. Cook to the desired doneness: about 5 to 6 minutes on each side for rare, 6 to 7 minutes on each

side for medium, and 9 to 10 minutes on each side for well-done. (This burger may also be cooked on a well-seasoned flat griddle or in a large nonstick sauté pan over medium-high heat. Cook for about the same amount of time as listed for grilling.)

Remove the burgers from the grill. Toast the buns, cut side down, on the grill or griddle or in a nonstick sauté pan until golden brown, about 1 minute.

Spread ½ tablespoon mayonnaise onto each burger bun half. Place 1 of the lettuce leaves on the bottom half of each bun, then top each with a burger, 2 of the tomato slices, 2 of the papaya slices, and the top half of the bun. Serve immediately accompanied by Tropical Fruit Salad.

Tropical Fruit Salad

Yields 4 servings

2 **tablespoons fresh coconut milk**
2 **tablespoons malt vinegar**
1 **tablespoon dark rum**
1 **tablespoon fresh lime juice**
¼ **teaspoon seeded and minced fresh jalapeño chile**
3 **tablespoons peanut oil**
1 **ripe medium papaya (about 2 pounds), peeled, seeded, and cut into large chunks**
1 **ripe medium mango, pitted, peeled, and cut into large chunks**
1 **ripe medium banana, peeled and sliced ¼ inch thick**
1 **kiwi, peeled and sliced ¼ inch thick**
½ **cup toasted cashews**
2 **tablespoons grated fresh coconut**
½ **teaspoon chopped fresh cilantro**

In a 3-quart stainless steel bowl, whisk together the coconut milk, malt vinegar, rum, lime juice, and jalapeños. Continue to whisk the mixture while pouring in a slow, steady stream of the peanut oil. Add the papaya, mango, banana, and kiwi to the dressing, and gently toss. Portion 1 cup of dressed fruits per serving, and garnish with the cashews, coconut, and cilantro. Serve immediately.

The dressed tropical fruits may be stored covered in the refrigerator for 2 to 3 days. Hold the cashews, coconut, and cilantro separately, and garnish just before serving.

Jumbo Lump Crabmeat Burger
with Marinated Red Cabbage Slaw

Makes 4 burgers

Rodney Stoner
Director of Food and Beverage
The Greenbrier Hotel
White Sulphur Springs, West Virginia

FOOD SERVICE HAS BEEN ROD STONER'S LIFE FROM THE TIME OF HIS EARLY TEENS, WHEN HE WORKED FOR HIS GRANDFATHER IN THE FAMILY CATERING BUSINESS. AFTER GRADUATING FROM THE CULINARY INSTITUTE OF AMERICA IN 1965, ROD WORKED AT THE BOAR'S HEAD INN IN CHARLOTTESVILLE, VIRGINIA. HE THEN BECAME A CULINARY APPRENTICE AT THE GREENBRIER BEFORE JOINING THE COLONIAL WILLIAMSBURG FOUNDATION.

ROD RETURNED TO THE GREENBRIER, ONE OF ONLY A HANDFUL OF OPERATIONS IN THE UNITED STATES BEARING THE MOBIL FIVE-STAR AND THE AMERICAN AUTOMOBILE ASSOCIATION FIVE-DIAMOND AWARDS, IN 1977. IN ADDITION TO BEING DIRECTOR OF FOOD AND BEVERAGE FOR THE GREENBRIER, HE ACTS AS VICE PRESIDENT OF FOOD AND BEVERAGE FOR THE GREENBRIER RESORT MANAGEMENT COMPANY, WHICH OWNS AND OPERATES OTHER RESORT PROPERTIES.

SINCE THE GREENBRIER RESORT USES OVER 10,000 POUNDS OF CRABMEAT PER YEAR, ROD THOUGHT A SPECIAL BURGER USING CRABMEAT WAS A NATURAL. THIS JUMBO LUMP CRABMEAT BURGER SHOULD MAKE A NOTEWORTHY ADDITION TO YOUR RECIPE FILE.

5 tablespoons unsalted butter
1/2 cup diced celery
1/2 cup thinly sliced scallions
  Salt and pepper to season
3 tablespoons mayonnaise
2 tablespoons sour cream
1 teaspoon Old Bay seasoning
1 teaspoon fresh lemon juice
1 pound fresh jumbo lump blue crabmeat, well picked of shell (see Note)
4 sourdough English muffins, split
4 1/4-ounce slices Muenster cheese
1/2 cup grated Asiago cheese (see Note)

Heat 1 tablespoon butter in a small nonstick sauté pan over medium-high heat. When hot, add the celery and sauté for 2 minutes. Add the scallions, lightly season with salt and pepper, and sauté for an additional minute. Transfer the celery and scallions to a dinner plate, and place uncovered in the refrigerator to cool.

In a 3-quart stainless steel bowl, whisk together the mayonnaise, sour cream, Old Bay seasoning, and lemon juice. Use a rubber spatula to fold in the cooled celery and scallions. Adjust the seasoning with salt and pepper, and combine thoroughly. Very gently fold in the crabmeat, being careful not to break up the pieces.

Gently form the crabmeat mixture into four 5-ounce, 1-inch-thick burgers. Cover the burgers with plastic wrap and refrigerate until needed.

Preheat the oven to the broil setting.

Heat 1 tablespoon butter in a large nonstick sauté pan over medium-high heat. When hot, pan-fry the crab burgers until golden brown, about 4 minutes on each side.

While the crab burgers are frying, toast the English muffins under the broiler or in a toaster. Spread the remaining 3 tablespoons butter onto the split sides of the toasted muffins.

Drink a pleasantly fruity
Chardonnay with your Jumbo Lump
Crabmeat Burger. The Williamsburg
Winery Act 12 Chardonnay would
do quite nicely.

Place the crab burgers on the buttered sides of 4 of the English muffin halves. Place a slice of the Muenster on top of each. Sprinkle each with one-fourth of the Asiago. Place on a baking sheet and brown the cheese under the broiler, about 2 to 3 minutes. Top with the other muffin halves and serve immediately accompanied by Marinated Red Cabbage Slaw.

Note: Although available virtually year-round, fresh jumbo lump blue crabmeat is at its best from April through late October. As the seasons change and the water temperature drops, the crabs make their way to the bottom and into the sand or mud, where they must be dredged up, resulting in lesser-quality crabmeat.

"Jumbo lump" refers to the two large pieces of white meat from the body of a cooked crab. This is the most expensive part of the blue crab, but quite assuredly the best. Less expensive backfin crabmeat may be used for this recipe; however, it will not deliver the same texturally pleasing qualities of the jumpo lump.

Asiago is a semi-hard, mildly flavored cheese produced both in Italy and in Wisconsin. Look for Asiago cheese in the supermarket or in a specialty cheese store.

Marinated Red Cabbage Slaw

Yields 4 servings

³/₄ **cup sherry wine vinegar**
¹/₂ **cup extra-virgin olive oil**
2 **tablespoons turbinado sugar (sugar in the raw)**
1 **tablespoon dry mustard**
1 **teaspoon celery seeds**
1 **teaspoon salt**
1 **teaspoon ground white pepper**
1 **medium head red cabbage, cored and sliced thin**
1 **medium onion, sliced thin**

Heat the sherry wine vinegar, olive oil, sugar, mustard, celery seeds, salt, and pepper in a 2-quart saucepan over high heat. Bring to a boil. Place the cabbage and onions in a 5-quart stainless steel bowl. Pour the boiling dressing over the cabbage and onions (do not stir), cover with plastic wrap, and marinate in the refrigerator for 4 to 6 hours. Toss the cabbage and onions together, and serve. The slaw may be stored tightly covered in a noncorrosive container for 2 to 3 days.

The slaw makes a vividly colorful
counterpoint to the prosaic appearance
of the burger. But more importantly,
it is a very tasty accompaniment.

Duck Burger

with Wild Rice Buns, Caramelized Sliced Onions, and Tarragon Mushrooms

Makes 4 burgers

Paul Sturkey
Chef/Owner
Pigall's Cafe
Cincinnati, Ohio

A NATIVE MIDWESTERNER, PAUL STURKEY GRADUATED FROM THE UNIVERSITY OF AKRON, IN AKRON, OHIO, BEFORE ATTENDING THE CULINARY INSTITUTE OF AMERICA.

CHEF STURKEY HAS COMPILED AN IMPRESSIVE LIST OF ACCOMPLISHMENTS SINCE HIS GRADUATION. FROM 1980 TO 1985 HE FOUNDED AND DEVELOPED THE GREATER CINCINNATI CULINARY ACADEMY, WHICH TRAINS COOKS WHO ASPIRE TO BECOME CHEFS. IN 1987, AS EXECUTIVE CHEF, HE OPENED THE RESTAURANT AT THE PHOENIX IN DOWNTOWN CINCINNATI, WHICH WAS CHOSEN THAT YEAR AS ONE OF THE TEN BEST NEW RESTAURANTS IN AMERICA BY *ESQUIRE* MAGAZINE. AND IN APRIL 1991, PAUL STURKEY REOPENED PIGALL'S, A HISTORIC LANDMARK RESTAURANT IN DOWNTOWN CINCINNATI THAT FOR OVER THIRTY YEARS HAD BEEN ONE OF THAT CITY'S TWO FIVE-STAR RESTAURANTS. RENAMED PIGALL'S CAFE, UNDER CHEF STURKEY'S MASTERFUL HAND, THE RESTAURANT HAS TAKEN CINCINNATI BY STORM, AND IN A VERY SHORT TIME IT HAS CREATED A NEW TRADITION IN CINCINNATI DINING.

½ cup chicken stock or water
2 teaspoons minced garlic
1½ pounds boneless and skinless duck breast meat, trimmed of fat and cut into 1-inch pieces (or 1½ pounds ground duck breast meat)
8 ounces diced pork fat
2 tablespoons chopped fresh sage
2 teaspoons chopped fresh tarragon
1 tablespoon salt
1 tablespoon freshly ground black pepper

Heat the chicken stock or water in a small saucepan over medium-high heat. Bring to a simmer. Poach the garlic in the simmering stock for 3 to 5 minutes. Strain the garlic and discard the stock. Transfer the garlic onto a small plate and place uncovered in the refrigerator to cool.

If using duck meat pieces, grind through a meat grinder fitted with a coarse grinding plate into a 5-quart stainless steel bowl.

Add the pork fat, chilled garlic, sage, tarragon, salt, and pepper to the ground duck meat. Gently but thoroughly combine.

Gently form the ground duck mixture into four 8-ounce, 1¼-inch-thick burgers. Cover the burgers with plastic wrap and refrigerate until needed.

Grill the burgers over a medium charcoal or wood fire. Cook until about medium, 8 to 9 minutes on each side. (This burger may also be cooked on a well-seasoned flat griddle or in a large nonstick sauté pan over medium-high heat. Cook for about the same amount of time as listed for grilling.)

Remove the burgers from the grill. Cut 4 Wild Rice Buns in half. Toast the buns, cut side down, on the grill or griddle or in a nonstick sauté pan until golden brown, about 45 seconds.

Serve the Duck Burgers on the buns, topped with Caramelized Sliced Onions and Tarragon Mushrooms.

Wild Rice Buns

Makes 8 buns

4   cups plus 1 tablespoon water
½   cup wild rice
1½ teaspoons salt
¾   cup milk
2   tablespoons unsalted butter
2   tablespoons cottage cheese
2   tablespoons granulated sugar
1   tablespoon active dry yeast
4   cups bread flour
1   cup finely diced onions
1   large egg yolk

Heat 4 cups water to a boil in a small saucepan.

Add the wild rice and ½ teaspoon salt. Adjust the heat to allow the rice to simmer slowly until each wild rice grain is completely open, about 1½ hours. Remove from the heat and drain in a colander. Allow the rice to cool to room temperature, about 10 to 15 minutes.

Heat the milk, butter, cottage cheese, sugar, and remaining 1 teaspoon salt in a 1½-quart saucepan over medium heat to a temperature of 120°F, approximately 4 minutes. Remove from the heat and pour into the bowl of an electric mixer. Add the yeast and stir gently to dissolve. Allow the mixture to stand and foam for 8 minutes.

Add 3½ cups flour, the cooked wild rice, and the onions. Combine on the low speed of an electric mixer fitted with a dough hook for 2 minutes. Scrape down the sides of the bowl, then continue to mix on low speed until the dough is thoroughly combined and smooth, about 5 minutes. (If a table-model electric mixer is not available, follow the directions using a hand-held mixer or kneading by hand. The mixing times will increase depending upon which alternative method is used.)

Remove the bowl from the mixer, and cover with a towel or plastic wrap. Allow the dough to rise in a warm location until it has doubled in volume, about 1 hour.

Place the dough on a clean, dry, lightly floured work surface, using the remaining ½ cup flour as necessary. Use a sharp knife to cut the dough into 8 equal portions. Shape each portion into a round ball. Divide the dough balls onto 2 baking sheets lined with parchment paper. Cover each baking sheet with plastic wrap and allow to rest for 10 minutes.

Preheat the oven to 350°F.

Slightly flatten each dough ball. Allow to rise in a warm location until doubled in size, about 20 to 25 minutes.

Whisk the egg yolk and remaining 1 tablespoon water, then lightly brush the top of each flattened dough ball with this egg wash.

Bake for 20 to 25 minutes, rotating the baking sheets from top to bottom and front to back about halfway through the baking time.

Allow the Wild Rice Buns to cool thoroughly before cutting in half.

The buns will keep fresh for 2 to 3 days stored in a resealable plastic bag at room temperature.

Considered by many to be quintessentially American food, wild rice, which is actually a grass and not a grain, lends a very specific flavor to this bun. The rice must be thoroughly cooked, that is, until each kernel has completely opened—or it will harden during the baking process.

Caramelized Sliced Onions

Yields 4 servings

**2 medium onions, cut into 8 ¹/₂-inch-thick
    slices**

Heat a large nonstick sauté pan over medium heat.
When the pan is hot, place the onion slices in the pan and
caramelize for 20 minutes on each side. The caramelized
onions may be used immediately or kept warm in a
200°F oven for up to 30 minutes before serving.

Tarragon Mushrooms

Yields 4 servings

4 tablespoons unsalted butter
¹/₄ cup dry white wine
1 tablespoon chopped fresh tarragon
**10 ounces fresh shiitake mushrooms, stems
    removed, sliced**

Heat the butter and white wine in a medium nonstick
sauté pan over medium-high heat. When the butter has
melted, add the tarragon and sauté for about 6 to 8 seconds. Add the shiitake mushrooms and sauté for 4 to 5
minutes. Serve immediately on the Duck Burgers.

*If you happen to be in Paul's
neighborhood, you should accompany
your burger with an Oldenberg
blond beer, brewed in Fort Wright,
Kentucky.*

*The aroma that wafts from the Duck
Burgers when they are grilling is sure
to seduce the olfactory receptors. This
is "outdoor" food at its best. Be
prepared to part with this recipe as
Paul Sturkey did, for once consumed,
this Duck Burger will be forever
remembered and craved.*

Aztec Burger

with Chocolate Buns, Rubblechuck Fries, and Raspberry Relish

Makes 4 burgers

John Twichell
Pastry Chef
The Trellis Restaurant
Williamsburg, Virginia

HOW DOES A PASTRY CHEF GET TANGLED UP IN A COOKBOOK ABOUT BURGERS? IT WAS NOT A MATTER OF BEING COERCED; RATHER, IT WAS A FEAR OF BEING LEFT OUT OF ALL THE FUN THAT PROMPTED JOHN TO SUGGEST THIS UNCONVENTIONAL BURGER.

JOHN TWICHELL HAS WORKED AT THE TRELLIS SINCE HE GRADUATED FROM THE CULINARY INSTITUTE OF AMERICA IN 1986. HE STARTED IN THE PANTRY, QUICKLY ADVANCING TO OTHER STATIONS. WITHIN A YEAR AND A HALF, HE WAS ASSISTANT PASTRY CHEF; HE BECAME PASTRY CHEF IN FEBRUARY 1988 AT THE AGE OF TWENTY-TWO.

ON A BUSY DAY, JOHN MASTERMINDS THE TRANSFORMATION OF FORTY TO FIFTY POUNDS OF CHOCOLATE INTO DECADENT DESSERTS SERVED TO CHOCOLATE LOVERS. JOHN IS ALSO RESPONSIBLE FOR THE DAILY PRODUCTION OF A VARIETY OF BREADS AND THE RENOWNED TRELLIS BREAD STICKS.

ALTHOUGH JOHN HAS GONE OVER THE TOP IN DEVISING HIS AZTEC BURGER, SO NAMED BECAUSE THE AZTECS WERE KNOWN TO OFFER AN UNSWEETENED CHOCOLATE DRINK TO THEIR VICTIMS OF HUMAN SACRIFICE, THIS CUNNING CONFECTIONER KNOWS NO OTHER WAY.

3/4 cup heavy cream
8 ounces semisweet chocolate, broken into 1/2-ounce pieces
2 ounces white chocolate, broken into 1/2-ounce pieces
8 1/4-inch-thick slices peeled kiwi
1/2 ounce finely grated white chocolate

Heat the heavy cream in a 1 1/2-quart saucepan over medium-high heat. Bring to a boil. Place the semisweet chocolate pieces in a 3-quart stainless steel bowl. Pour the boiling cream over the chocolate and allow to stand for 5 minutes. Stir with a whisk until smooth. Use a rubber spatula to scrape the sides of the bowl. Whisk again to ensure that there are no lumps. Pour the mixture onto a baking sheet with sides and refrigerate until firm but not hard, about 35 minutes.

Draw 4 circles, approximately 3 1/2 inches in diameter, onto a sheet of parchment paper (the pencil lines should be dark enough to show through the paper). Place the paper, penciled side down, onto a clean baking sheet. Use a rubber spatula to scrape the chilled chocolate from the baking sheet into a pastry bag fitted with a small star tip.

Fill the traced parchment circles with the chilled chocolate, starting in the center and piping toward the outside of each circle to form 1/2-inch-thick "burgers."

Place the baking sheet of formed burgers in the freezer until very firm, about 30 minutes. Cover the burgers with plastic wrap and refrigerate until needed.

Make the white chocolate "cheese slices" for the burgers. Heat 1 inch water in the bottom half of a double boiler over low heat. Place the 2 ounces white chocolate pieces in the top half of the double boiler. Using a rubber spatula, constantly stir the white chocolate until melted, about 4 minutes. Remove the chocolate from the heat, and continue stirring until the chocolate reaches a temperature of 84 to 86°F, about 3 minutes.

125

Cover the bottom of a baking sheet with plastic wrap, using your hands to smooth out the wrinkles. Pour the melted white chocolate onto the baking sheet and spread it to a square measuring 7 by 7 inches. Refrigerate until firm but not hard, about 3 minutes. Cut the white chocolate into 4 equal 3½-inch squares. Refrigerate the squares until completely hardened, about 10 minutes.

Remove the burgers from the parchment paper and place on the bottom halves of the Chocolate Buns. Place 1 slice of the white chocolate "cheese" on top of each burger, then place 2 of the kiwi slices (for the pickles) on top of the white chocolate "cheese." Top with the top bun halves. Sprinkle the finely grated white chocolate (for the sesame seeds, of course) over the top of each bun, and serve accompanied by Rubblechuck Fries and Raspberry Relish.

Chocolate Buns

Makes 4 buns

¾ cup plus 1 tablespoon all-purpose flour
3 tablespoons unsweetened cocoa
½ teaspoon baking soda
½ teaspoon salt
4 tablespoons plus 2 teaspoons unsalted butter, softened
1 ounce unsweetened chocolate, chopped into ¼-inch pieces
½ cup tightly packed light brown sugar
1 large egg
½ teaspoon vanilla extract
½ teaspoon red raspberry vinegar
½ cup boiling water

Preheat the oven to 325°F.

Sift together ¾ cup flour and the cocoa, baking soda, and salt onto waxed paper, and set aside until needed.

Lightly coat four 8-ounce ovenproof soufflé cups with 2 teaspoons butter. Dust the insides with the remaining 1 tablespoon flour. Shake out any excess flour.

Heat 1 inch water in the bottom half of a double boiler over medium heat. Place the unsweetened chocolate in the top half of the double boiler. Tightly cover the top with plastic wrap. Allow to heat for 2 to 3 minutes. Remove from the heat and stir until smooth. Set aside until needed.

Place the brown sugar and remaining 4 tablespoons butter into the bowl of an electric mixer fitted with a paddle. Beat on medium speed for 1 minute, then on high for 1 minute. Scrape down the sides of the bowl, then beat for an additional minute. Scrape down the sides of the bowl, then add the egg and beat on high for 30 seconds. Add the vanilla extract and red raspberry vinegar, and beat on high for 20 seconds. Add the melted unsweetened chocolate and mix on low speed for 10 seconds. Scrape down the sides of the bowl. Now add the sifted dry ingredients and mix on low for 10 seconds.

Increase the speed to medium and beat for 10 seconds. Adjust the speed to low, add the boiling water, and continue to mix for 10 seconds. Remove the bowl from the mixer. Use a rubber spatula to mix the batter until smooth and thoroughly combined. (If a table-model electric mixer is not available, follow the directions using a hand-held mixer or mixing by hand. The mixing times will increase depending upon which alternative method is used.)

Evenly divide the batter among the 4 prepared soufflé cups. Bake in the center of the oven until a toothpick inserted into the center of a "bun" comes out clean, about 22 to 25 minutes. Remove from the oven and allow to cool in the cups for 10 minutes. Remove the "buns" from the cups, place upright on a dinner plate, and while still warm, wrap tightly with plastic wrap. Allow to stand at room temperature for at least 1 hour.

Use a very sharp serrated knife or slicer to cut the buns in half horizontally.

The buns are at their best when served at room temperature. They may be refrigerated for 2 to 3 days; remove from the refrigerator about 2 hours before using.

Rubblechuck Fries

Yields 4 servings

1 cup all-purpose flour
3 tablespoons unsalted butter
3 tablespoons water
1 large egg yolk
½ cup granulated sugar
1½ teaspoons unsweetened cocoa
½ teaspoon cinnamon

> Rubblechuck *is a slang kitchen term from England for piecrust odds and ends that are rolled with sugar and cinnamon and baked as a special treat for youngsters. Whatever your age, John believes you will love his adaptation.*

Combine the flour and butter in the bowl of an electric mixer fitted with a paddle. Mix on medium speed until the butter is "cut into" the flour, about 2 minutes. Add the water and egg yolk, and continue to mix on medium speed for 30 seconds. Remove the dough from the mixer and form it into a smooth ball. Wrap tightly with plastic wrap and refrigerate for 1 hour. (If a table-model electric mixer is not available, follow the directions using a hand-held mixer or kneading by hand. The mixing times will increase depending upon which alternative method is used.)

Preheat the oven to 325°F.

Lightly sprinkle a clean, dry work surface with some of the sugar. Place the dough on the surface; use a rolling pin to roll the dough into a circle about 6 inches in diameter and ½ inch thick. Sprinkle the cocoa and cinnamon evenly over the dough, and roll into a circle 12 inches in diameter and ⅛ inch thick (using more sugar as necessary to prevent the dough from sticking). Fold the dough in half, and roll (using more sugar as necessary to prevent the dough from sticking) into a 16- by 10-inch rounded shape that is ⅛ inch thick. Fold and roll once again (using more sugar as necessary to prevent the dough from sticking) into a 16- by 6-inch rectangular shape that is ⅛ inch thick. At this point, all the sugar should have been used.

Use a sharp knife to cut the dough into ¼-inch-wide strips. Line 2 baking sheets with parchment paper. Lay the strips of dough ¼ inch apart on the baking sheets. Bake for 10 to 12 minutes. Remove from the oven and cool to room temperature. Store the fries in an airtight container to retain crispness.

Raspberry Relish

Yields 4 servings

¼ cup water
¼ cup granulated sugar
¼ teaspoon minced orange zest
1½ cups fresh or individually quick-frozen raspberries
1 teaspoon fresh orange juice

Heat the water, sugar, and orange zest in a 1½-quart saucepan over medium-high heat. Bring to a boil and allow to boil until slightly thickened, about 3 to 4 minutes. Stir in ½ cup raspberries and continue to boil for 2 minutes.

Remove from the heat and strain into a small stainless steel bowl. Discard the seeds. Immediately add the remaining 1 cup raspberries and orange juice. Stir to combine. Refrigerate for at least 30 minutes before serving.

The raspberry relish will keep, tightly covered in a noncorrosive container, for 2 to 3 days.

> *This relish also makes a great topping for ice cream.*

Buffalo Burger

with Piquant Avocado; Onion, Sage, and Mustard Relish; and Fresh Sage Tortillas

Makes 4 burgers

Carl E. Walker

Executive Chef
Brennan's
Houston, Texas

BORN IN FAYETTE, MISSOURI, CHEF CARL WALKER DEVELOPED A PASSION FOR FOOD AND COOKING WHILE GROWING UP ON HIS PARENTS' FARM. THE PRESENCE OF FRESH GAME AND PRODUCE, COMBINED WITH HIS MOTHER'S TALENT IN THE KITCHEN, INSPIRED CARL TO BEGIN EXPLORING THE ART OF COOKING. HE BEGAN HIS FORMAL TRAINING IN THE U.S. MARINE CORPS' COOK'S SCHOOL, WHERE HE GRADUATED FIRST IN HIS CLASS. CARL COMPLETED HIS FORMAL EDUCATION AT THE CULINARY INSTITUTE OF AMERICA.

WITH CHEF CARL WALKER BEHIND THE STOVE, BRENNAN'S HAS RECEIVED A NUMBER OF NOTABLE AWARDS, INCLUDING THE HONOR OF BEING THE FIRST TEXAS RESTAURANT TO RECEIVE *RESTAURANTS AND INSTITUTIONS* MAGAZINE'S PRESTIGIOUS IVY AWARD.

One good mail-order source of institutional and retail cuts of buffalo meat is:
Rocky Mountain Natural Meats
P.O. Box 16668
Denver, CO 80216
(800) 327-2706

2 pounds ground buffalo meat (see Note)
1 cup minced onions
1 jalapeño chile, roasted, skinned, seeded, and minced
2 teaspoons salt
1 teaspoon freshly ground black pepper
4 ½-ounce slices smoked Monterey Jack cheese
2 tablespoons vegetable oil
8 slices ripe red tomatoes

In a 5-quart stainless steel bowl, gently but thoroughly combine the ground buffalo meat, onions, jalapeños, salt, and pepper.

Gently form the seasoned meat into four 8½-ounce, 1¼-inch-thick burgers. Cover the burgers with plastic wrap and refrigerate until needed.

Grill the burgers over a medium wood or charcoal fire. Cook to the desired doneness: about 5 to 6 minutes on each side for rare, 7 to 8 minutes on each side for medium, and 10 to 12 minutes on each side for well-done. Top each burger with a slice of the smoked Monterey Jack and allow to melt. If you have a cover for the grill, quickly melt the cheese by placing it over the grill for a few moments. (This burger may also be cooked on a well-seasoned flat griddle or in a large nonstick sauté pan over medium-high heat. Cook for about the same amount of time as listed for grilling.)

Remove the burgers from the grill. Lightly brush 8 Fresh Sage Tortillas on 1 side with the vegetable oil. Toast the tortillas, oil side down, on the grill or griddle or in a nonstick sauté pan until lightly browned but still soft, about 2 minutes.

Spread 2 tablespoons Piquant Avocado onto the grilled side of 4 of the tortillas. Then top each with 2 of the tomato slices and a Buffalo Burger. Garnish the top of each burger with 1 tablespoon Onion, Sage, and Mustard Relish. Place another tortilla, grilled side up, on top. Cut each burger into quarters and serve.

Note: Look for buffalo meat in large supermarkets or through mail-order sources.

Piquant Avocado

Yields 1⅓ cups

2 ripe avocados
1 lemon
1 small jalapeño chile, roasted, skinned, seeded, and minced
¾ teaspoon finely chopped fresh cilantro
2 dashes Tabasco Sauce
  Salt and pepper to season

Cut, pit, and peel the avocados. Cut the avocado pulp into large pieces. Place the avocado pieces into a stainless steel bowl and use the back of a dinner fork to mash them to a coarse texture. Squeeze the juice of the lemon over the mashed avocados. Add the jalapeños, cilantro, and Tabasco Sauce to the mashed avocados. Season with salt and pepper. Use a rubber spatula and gently stir to combine. Serve immediately. The Piquant Avocado may be kept covered in the refrigerator for several hours.

Onion, Sage, and Mustard Relish

Yields ½ cup

1½ teaspoons olive oil
1 large onion, sliced thin
½ cup cider vinegar
4 tablespoons granulated sugar
1 tablespoon Dijon mustard
2 teaspoons finely chopped fresh sage
  Salt and pepper to season

Heat the olive oil in a medium sauté pan over medium-high heat. When hot, add the onions and cook until translucent, about 4 minutes. Add the cider vinegar and sugar, and continue cooking, stirring frequently, until the mixture becomes thick and starts to brown lightly, about 15 to 20 minutes. Remove from the heat and stir in the mustard and sage. Season with salt and pepper, and serve immediately.

The relish may be kept warm in a double boiler for up to 1 hour before serving.

To keep the relish for several days, first cool in an ice-water bath, then transfer to a noncorrosive storage container, cover, and refrigerate. Heat until warm before serving.

Fresh Sage Tortillas

Makes 8 Tortillas

2 cups all-purpose flour
2 teaspoons baking powder
2 teaspoons salt
1 teaspoon minced fresh sage
1 tablespoon vegetable shortening
½ cup plus 6 tablespoons warm water

In a 5-quart stainless steel bowl, sift together the flour, baking powder, and salt. Stir in the sage. Cut the shortening into the dry ingredients, and work it in with your hands until the mixture is the consistency of coarse cornmeal.

Make a well in the center of the flour mixture and add ½ cup warm water. Use a rubber spatula to work the flour in from the sides (add an additional 1 to 6 tablespoons water as needed to get the dough to come together). Gently knead the dough with your hands until it forms a smooth ball.

Cover the bowl with plastic wrap and allow the dough to rest at room temperature for 1 hour.

Remove the dough from the bowl and place it on a lightly floured cutting board. Use a sharp knife to cut the dough into eight 2-ounce pieces. Gently form the pieces into balls, cover loosely with plastic wrap, and allow to rest for an additional 15 minutes.

Use a wooden rolling pin to roll each ball into a tortilla about 5 inches in diameter. Wrap the tortillas with plastic wrap and refrigerate until ready to cook. The raw tortillas may be kept refrigerated for up to 4 days.

Mediterranean Lamb Burger
with Tomato and Red Pepper Chutney

Makes 6 burgers

Joseph Weissenberg
Senior Chef-Instructor
The Culinary Institute of America
Hyde Park, New York

SINCE GRADUATING FROM THE CULINARY INSTITUTE OF AMERICA, JOSEPH WEISSENBERG HAS CRISSCROSSED AMERICA WORKING IN CULINARY LANDMARKS, INCLUDING THE GOLDEN LAMB HOTEL IN LEBANON, OHIO, WHERE HE WAS EXECUTIVE CHEF.

HIS PROUDEST MOMENT, HOWEVER, WAS IN EUROPE IN 1976, WHEN, AS A MEMBER OF THE INSTITUTE'S ALUMNI TEAM, HE WON FIVE GOLD MEDALS AT THE SALON CULINAIRE MONDIAL IN BASEL, SWITZERLAND.

THE SIMPLICITY OF JOSEPH'S MEDITERRANEAN LAMB BURGER BELIES ITS INTENSITY OF FLAVOR.

> *Selecting a beverage to measure up to the hearty flavor of Joseph's lamb burger may not be as formidable a task as one might imagine. Reflect on the Mediterranean geography that inspired this burger, and you may find yourself in the Piedmont region of Italy, sipping a brawny yet satisfying Barbaresco in between bites of this delicious burger.*

2 pounds fresh lamb meat from shoulder, trimmed and cut into 1-inch pieces (or 2 pounds ground lamb meat from shoulder)
1 teaspoon salt
1 teaspoon coarsely ground black pepper
6 whole wheat pita breads
1 teaspoon extra-virgin olive oil
1 small head curly endive, cut into ³/₄-inch pieces, washed, and dried

If using lamb pieces, grind through a meat grinder fitted with a coarse grinding plate into a 5-quart stainless steel bowl.

Gently but thoroughly combine the ground lamb with the salt and pepper.

Gently form the seasoned lamb into six 5-ounce, 1-inch-thick burgers. Cover the burgers with plastic wrap and refrigerate until needed.

Preheat the oven to 275°F.

Place the pita breads on a baking sheet and heat in the oven. When hot, lower the oven temperature to its lowest setting, and hold the pita breads warm while grilling the lamb burgers.

Lightly brush the burgers with the olive oil.

Grill the burgers over a medium wood or charcoal fire. Cook to the desired doneness: 3 to 4 minutes on each side for rare, 5 to 6 minutes on each side for medium, and 8 to 9 minutes on each side for well-done. (This burger may also be cooked on a well-seasoned flat griddle or in a large nonstick sauté pan over medium-high heat. Cook for about the same amount of time as listed for grilling.)

Remove the pita breads from the oven. Cut a 1³/₄-inch piece from the top of each pita bread, and gently split open the bread. Stuff each pita with curly endive and a lamb burger. Spoon 2 or 3 teaspoons Tomato and Red Pepper Chutney directly onto the meat. Serve immediately.

Tomato and Red Pepper Chutney

Yields 1½ cups

2 tablespoons olive oil
4 scallions, trimmed and sliced thin
1 small red bell pepper, seeded and cut into
    ½-inch dice
1 clove garlic, minced
2 large tomatoes, peeled, seeded, and chopped
⅛ teaspoon ground coriander
⅛ teaspoon ground cumin
⅛ teaspoon ground nutmeg
⅛ teaspoon ground turmeric
    Pinch cayenne pepper
1 tablespoon cider vinegar
1 tablespoon granulated sugar
1 tablespoon tomato paste
    Salt and cayenne pepper to season

This condiment is as versatile as your culinary imagination. It works delightfully well with other meats, poultry, and even creatures of the deep—it is terrific served chilled with steamed shrimp. Experiment with its serving temperature; it is delicious yet subtly different when served chilled, warm, or at room temperature.

Heat the olive oil in a 2½-quart stainless steel saucepan over medium heat. When hot, add the scallions, red bell peppers, and garlic. Sauté for 2 minutes.

Add the tomatoes and sauté for an additional 2 minutes.

Add the ground spices and pinch cayenne pepper and combine thoroughly. Add the cider vinegar and sugar, and cook for an additional 2 minutes, occasionally stirring to prevent the mixture from scorching.

Add the tomato paste and combine thoroughly. Allow the mixture to simmer for 15 minutes. Remove the chutney from the heat. Adjust the seasoning with salt and additional cayenne pepper, depending on the intensity of heat you prefer.

Cool the chutney in an ice-water bath until cold. Refrigerate the chutney in a stainless steel or other non-corrosive container. Keep refrigerated for 12 hours before serving (this allows the flavors to commingle).

The chutney will keep tightly covered in the refrigerator for up to 2 weeks. You can also make large batches of this chutney, canning what will not be used within a few days.

Venison Burger

Makes 4 burgers

Jasper White
Chef/Owner
Restaurant Jasper
Boston, Massachusetts

JASPER WHITE HAS ALWAYS BEEN A SUPPORTER OF "THE BASICS OF COOKING." FOR EXAMPLE, HE CONSIDERS A SIMPLE ROASTED CHICKEN AS THE BENCHMARK FOR UNDERSTANDING THE PREPARATION OF GOOD FOOD. AT HIS CELEBRATED RESTAURANT IN BOSTON, JASPER HAS CRAFTED A STYLE OF COOKING THAT HONORS THE BASICS, YET FAR TRANSCENDS THE ORDINARY.

JASPER, THE AUTHOR OF *JASPER WHITE'S COOKING FROM NEW ENGLAND,* HAS BECOME A SELF-APPOINTED SPOKESMAN FOR THE OFTEN MISUNDERSTOOD AND MISINTERPRETED COOKING OF NEW ENGLAND. HIS VENISON BURGER REFLECTS HIS LONG INTEREST IN HUNTING AND HIS RESPECT FOR NEW ENGLAND'S CUISINE.

Although the Venison Burgers are delicious with the condiments recommended above, Jasper suggests that diners "fix up their own burgers" in their own individual ways. Another suggestion from Jasper is to have plenty of Bass ale on hand.

1¼ **pounds trimmed venison from shoulder or leg, cut into 1-inch cubes (or 1¼ pounds ground trimmed venison from shoulder or leg)**
1 **tablespoon unsalted butter**
½ **cup diced onions**
¼ **pound diced pork fat**
1 **tablespoon olive oil**

Kosher salt and coarsely ground black pepper to season
4 **Onion Rolls (see page 89), cut in half**
Thinly sliced red onions
Sliced sour pickles
Spicy Dijon mustard
Sweet pepper relish
Tomato and Red Pepper Chutney (see page 133)

If using venison pieces, grind through a meat grinder fitted with a coarse grinding plate into a 5-quart stainless steel bowl. Cover the bowl with plastic wrap and refrigerate until needed.

Heat the butter in a small nonstick sauté pan over medium-high heat. When the butter is hot, add the onions, and sauté until translucent, about 3 to 4 minutes. Transfer the onions to a dinner plate and place uncovered in the refrigerator to cool.

Gently but thoroughly combine the ground venison with the pork fat and cooled onions.

Gently form the meat-onion mixture into four 6-ounce, 1-inch-thick burgers. Cover the burgers with plastic wrap and refrigerate until needed.

Prior to grilling, brush the Venison Burgers with the olive oil, and generously season with kosher salt and pepper.

Grill the burgers over a medium wood or charcoal fire. Cook to the desired doneness: 3 to 4 minutes on each side for medium rare, 5 to 6 minutes on each side for medium, and 8 to 9 minutes on each side for well-done. (This burger may also be cooked on a well-seasoned flat griddle or in a large nonstick sauté pan over medium-high heat. Cook for about the same amount of time as listed for grilling.)

Remove the burgers from the grill. Toast the rolls, cut side down, on the grill or griddle or in a nonstick sauté pan until golden brown, about 1 minute. Place each burger on the bottom half of a roll.

Top the burgers with the red onion slices, sour pickle slices, mustard, sweet pepper relish, Tomato and Red Pepper Chutney, and top bun halves.

Chili Grill Burger

with Jalapeño Cheddar Buns, Chipotle Mayonnaise, and Grilled Vegetables Prickly Pear

Makes 4 burgers

Alan Zeman
Executive Chef
Sheraton El Conquistador Resort
Tucson, Arizona

CONSIDERED BY MANY TO BE TUCSON'S AMBASSADOR OF SOUTHWEST CUISINE, ALAN ZEMAN HAS BEEN HOOKED ON THE CITY'S SUNSHINE AND MOUNTAINS SINCE HE MOVED THERE TO ATTEND THE UNIVERSITY OF ARIZONA IN 1975. WHILE STUDYING POLITICAL SCIENCE AT COLLEGE, HE WORKED HIS WAY THROUGH THE FINER HOTELS AND RESTAURANTS OF THE TUCSON AREA. FINDING THAT HE HAD A GREATER AFFINITY FOR THE KITCHEN THAN FOR POLITICAL SCIENCE, ALAN DECIDED TO ATTEND THE CULINARY INSTITUTE OF AMERICA.

AS ONE OF THE ARCHITECTS OF THE NEW SOUTHWEST CUISINE, ALAN DEVELOPED THE ORIGINAL PRICKLY PEAR BARBECUE GLAZE, MARKETED HIS OWN SONORAN SEASONING, AND IS WIDELY REGARDED AS THE INVENTOR OF THE DESSERT TACO.

ALAN'S CHILI GRILL BURGER BRINGS THE SOUTHWEST RIGHT TO THE PALATE.

To purchase Sonoran Seasoning spice blend directly from the source, write to:
Chef Alan Zeman's
Southwestern
Originals
P.O. Box 31283
Tucson, AZ 85751

---

2 **pounds ground beef chuck**
1 **tablespoon Sonoran Seasoning spice blend or favorite seasoned salt**
4 **large Anaheim chiles, roasted, skinned, and seeded**

4 **1-ounce slices Monterey Jack cheese with jalapeño (see Note)**
4 **iceberg lettuce leaves, washed and dried**
4 **¼-inch-thick slices ripe large tomatoes**

Gently form the ground beef into four 8-ounce, 1¼-inch-thick burgers. Cover the burgers with plastic wrap and refrigerate until needed.

Generously season the burgers with the Sonoran Seasoning or seasoned salt. Grill the burgers over a medium wood or charcoal fire. Cook to the desired doneness: 3 to 4 minutes on each side for rare, 6 to 7 minutes on each side for medium, and 8 to 9 minutes on each side for well-done. (This burger may also be cooked on a well-seasoned flat griddle or in a large nonstick sauté pan. Cook for about the same amount of time as listed for grilling.) As soon as the burgers have been cooked on one side and are turned, place 2 of the Anaheim chile halves on the grilled side of each burger, and then place a slice of the Monterey Jack on the chiles. Finish cooking to the desired doneness.

Remove the burgers from the grill. Cut 4 Jalapeño Cheddar Buns in half. Toast the buns on the grill or griddle or in a nonstick sauté pan, cut side down, until golden brown, about 1 minute. Place the burgers on the bottom bun halves and top with the lettuce and tomatoes. Spread the top bun halves with 1 tablespoon Chipotle Mayonnaise and place on top of the burgers. Serve immediately with Grilled Vegetables Prickly Pear.

Note: For an excellent Monterey Jack cheese with jalapeño, check your supermarket for Heluva Good brand cheese; besides tasting darn good, it is made without preservatives.

Jalapeño Cheddar Buns

Makes 12 buns

2	**cups milk**
2	**tablespoons granulated sugar**
2	**teaspoons salt**
2	**tablespoons active dry yeast**
6½	**cups bread flour**
9	**ounces grated cheddar cheese**
2	**large eggs**
¼	**cup plus 1 teaspoon vegetable oil**
3	**medium jalapeño chiles, stemmed, seeded, and minced**

Heat the milk, sugar, and salt in a 1½-quart saucepan over medium heat to a temperature of 120°F, about 4 to 5 minutes. Remove from the heat and pour into the bowl of an electric mixer. Add the yeast and stir gently to dissolve. Allow the mixture to stand and foam for 4 to 5 minutes.

Add 6 cups flour, 8 ounces cheddar, the eggs, ¼ cup vegetable oil, and the jalapeños. Place the mixing bowl on an electric mixer fitted with a dough hook. Mix on low speed for 1 minute. Stop the mixer, scrape down the sides of the bowl, and continue mixing on medium-low speed until the dough forms a smooth ball that pulls away from the sides of the bowl, about 4 to 5 minutes. (If a table-model electric mixer is not available, follow the directions using a hand-held mixer or kneading by hand. The mixing times will increase depending upon which alternative method is used.)

Coat the inside of a 5-quart stainless steel bowl with the remaining teaspoon vegetable oil. Place the dough in the bowl and wipe the bowl with the dough. Cover with plastic wrap. Allow the dough to rise in a warm location until it has doubled in size, about 1 hour.

Preheat the oven to 325°F.

Place the dough on a clean, dry, lightly floured work surface, using the remaining flour as necessary. Use a sharp knife to cut the dough into 12 equal portions. Shape each portion into a ball. Divide the balls onto 2 baking sheets lined with parchment paper. Slightly flatten the top of each ball. Loosely cover the dough with plastic wrap and allow to rise in a warm location until doubled in size, about 20 minutes.

When the buns have doubled in size, use a razor blade or a very sharp paring knife to cut a ½-inch-deep slit in the top of each bun. Sprinkle the remaining cheddar over the top of the buns. Bake the buns in the center of the oven for 23 to 25 minutes, until golden brown.

Allow the buns to cool thoroughly before cutting in half.

The rolls will keep fresh for 2 to 3 days at room temperature stored in a resealable plastic bag.

Chipotle Mayonnaise

Yields a bit more than 1 cup

2 small dried chipotle chiles, stemmed and seeded (see Note)
1 cup mayonnaise
1 tablespoon white wine Worcestershire sauce
1 teaspoon Sonoran Seasoning spice blend or favorite seasoned salt
1 teaspoon minced garlic

Use the edge of a cook's knife to press the chipotle chiles into a paste (this should yield about 1 teaspoon paste).

In a stainless steel bowl, whisk together the mayonnaise, chipotle paste, Worcestershire sauce, Sonoran Seasoning or seasoned salt, and garlic. Use immediately, or cover with plastic wrap and refrigerate for up to 2 days.

Note: Look for chipotle peppers in specialty grocery stores. The chipotle is actually a jalapeño that has been smoked. Although it is available in a can (immersed in a tomato-based sauce), the dried form should be purchased for this recipe.

Alan Zeman describes his Prickly Pear Barbecue Glaze as "a magenta-colored sauce with a base of prickly pear fruit and a blend of other tantalizing ingredients. The perfect sauce for grilled seafood, poultry, and vegetables..."

To purchase Prickly Pear Barbecue Glaze directly from the source, write to:
Chef Alan Zeman's Southwestern Originals
P.O. Box 31283
Tucson, AZ 85751

Grilled Vegetables Prickly Pear

Yields 4 servings

1 medium zucchini, washed and cut into 1/4-inch-thick diagonal slices
1 medium yellow squash, washed and cut into 1/4-inch-thick diagonal slices
1 medium eggplant, washed and cut into 1/4-inch-thick diagonal slices
8 scallions, trimmed
1/4 cup extra-virgin olive oil
2 tablespoons Sonoran Seasoning spice blend or favorite seasoned salt
3/4 cup Prickly Pear Barbecue Glaze, Quick Barbecue Sauce (see page 46), or a favorite barbecue sauce

Prior to grilling, brush the vegetables with the olive oil and season generously with the Sonoran Seasoning or seasoned salt. Grill the zucchini and yellow squash over a medium wood or charcoal fire for about 1 1/2 minutes on each side. Grill the eggplant for 45 to 60 seconds on each side. Grill the whole scallions quickly, about 30 seconds.

Transfer the grilled vegetables to a serving platter; brush liberally with the Prickly Pear Barbecue Glaze or barbecue sauce. Serve immediately.

The grilled vegetables may be kept warm in a 200°F oven for up to 30 minutes before serving. The vegetables are also good at room temperature; cover with plastic wrap and hold for up to 1 hour at room temperature before serving.

The Burger Meisters

Ms. Alison Awerbuch, Class of 1985
Corporate Executive Chef and Partner
Abigail Kirsch at Tappan Hill
81 Highland Avenue
Tarrytown, New York 10591

Mr. Benjamin Barker, Class of 1981
Chef/Proprietor
Magnolia Grill
1002 9th Street
Durham, North Carolina 27705

Ms. Elaine Bell, Class of 1978
Chef/Owner
Elaine Bell Catering Company
682 West Napa Street
Sonoma, California 95476

Ms. Carlyn Berghoff, Class of 1982
President/Owner
Carlyn Berghoff Catering
2nd Floor
125 North Wabash Avenue
Chicago, Illinois 60602

Mr. John Bowen, Class of 1973
Executive Vice President
Johnson & Wales University
8 Abbott Park Place
Providence, Rhode Island 02903

Ms. Lyde Buchtenkirch-Biscardi,
   C.M.C., Class of 1972
Team Leader for Curriculum
The Culinary Institute of America
433 Albany Post Road
Hyde Park, New York 12538-1499

Mr. David Burke, Class of 1982
Chef/Owner
Park Avenue Cafe
100 East 63rd Street
New York, New York 10021

Mr. Bill Cardwell, Class of 1971
Chef/Co-owner
Cardwell's
8100 Maryland Avenue
St. Louis, Missouri 63105

Mr. Michael Chiarello, Class of 1982
Chef/Owner
Tra Vigne
1050 Charter Oak
St. Helena, California 94574

Mr. Richard Czack, C.M.C.,
   Class of 1958
Executive Assistant to the
   Vice President of Education
The Culinary Institute of America
433 Albany Post Road
Hyde Park, New York 12538-1499

Mr. Edward Daggers, Class of 1985
Executive Chef
The Kingsmill Resort and
   Conference Center
1010 Kingsmill Road
Williamsburg, Virginia 23185

Mr. Sanford J. D'Amato, C.E.C.,
   Class of 1974
Chef/Owner
Sanford Restaurant
1547 North Jackson Street
Milwaukee, Wisconsin 53202

Mr. Marcel Desaulniers, C.E.C.,
   Class of 1965
Executive Chef/Co-owner
The Trellis Restaurant
403 Duke of Gloucester Street
Williamsburg, Virginia 23185

Mr. Robert Dickson, Class of 1963
Chef/Owner
Robert's of Charleston
112 North Market Streeet
Charleston, South Carolina 29401

Mr. John Doherty, Class of 1978
Executive Chef
The Waldorf-Astoria
301 Park Avenue
New York, New York 10022

Mr. Mark Erickson, C.M.C.,
   Class of 1977
Executive Chef
Cherokee Town & Country Club
155 West Paces Ferry Road
Atlanta, Georgia 30363

Mr. Dean Fearing, Class of 1978
Chef
The Mansion on Turtle Creek
2821 Turtle Creek Boulevard
Dallas, Texas 75219

Ms. Phyllis Flaherty-Bologna,
   C.E.C., C.C.E., Class of 1974
Executive Chef for National
   Accounts Development
General Foods Foodservice
250 North Street E G-3
White Plains, New York 10625

Mr. Larry Forgione, Class of 1974
Chef/Owner
An American Place
2 Park Avenue
New York, New York 10016

Ms. Jacqueline Frazer, Class of 1984
Personal Caterer
New York, New York

Mr. Kevin Garvin, Class of 1978
Executive Chef
The Adolphus Hotel
1321 Commerce Street
Dallas, Texas 75202

Mr. John A. Halligan, Class of 1982
Executive Chef
Halcyon Restaurant
Rihga Royal Hotel
151 West 54th Street
New York, New York 10019

Ms. Stephanie Hersh, Class of 1985
Assistant
Julia Child Productions
Cambridge, Massachusetts

Mr. James Heywood, Class of 1967
Chef-Instructor
The Culinary Institute of America
433 Albany Post Road
Hyde Park, New York 12538-1499

Mrs. Liz Heywood, Class of 1974
Chef-Instructor
The Culinary Institute of America
433 Albany Post Road
Hyde Park, New York 12538-1499

Mr. Gerry Klaskala, Class of 1976
Chef/Managing Partner
The Buckhead Diner
3073 Piedmont Road
Atlanta, Georgia 30305

Ms. Jenifer Lang, Class of 1978
Managing Director/Owner
Cafe des Artistes
One West 67th
New York, New York 10023

Mr. Daniel Leader, Class of 1976
Owner/Baker
Bread Alone, Inc.
Route 28
Boiceville, New York 12412

Mr. Vinnie Oakes, Class of 1965
Vice President of Food and Beverage
Desert Inn Hotel and Country Club
3145 Las Vegas Boulevard South
Las Vegas, Nevada 89109

Mr. Charles Palmer, Class of 1979
Executive Chef/Owner
Aureole
34 East 61st Street
New York, New York 10021

Mr. Jon Pierre Peavey, Class of 1988
Assistant Chef
The Trellis Restaurant
403 Duke of Gloucester Street
Williamsburg, Virginia 23185

John and Caprial Pence, Class of 1984
Chefs/Owners
Westmoreland Bistro and Wines
7015 S. E. Milwaukie
Portland, Oregon 97202

Ms. Nicole Routhier, Class of 1985
Cookbook Author
New York, New York

Mr. L. Timothy Ryan, C.M.C.,
   Class of 1977
Vice President of Education
The Culinary Institute of America
433 Albany Post Road
Hyde Park, New York 12538-1499

Mr. Charles Saunders, Class of 1978
Executive Chef/Owner
East Side Oyster Bar & Grill
133 East Napa Street
Sonoma, California 95476

Mr. Chris Schlesinger, Class of 1977
Chef/Owner
East Coast Grill
1271 Cambridge Street
Cambridge, Massachusetts 02139

Mr. Jamie Shannon, Class of 1984
Executive Chef
Commander's Palace
1403 Washington Avenue
New Orleans, Louisiana 70130

Mr. Arnym Solomon, Class of 1969
Vice President of Chain Accounts
CPC Foodservice
9353 Belmont Avenue
Franklin Park, Illinois 60131

Mr. Rodney Stoner, Class of 1965
Director of Food and Beverage
The Greenbrier Hotel
White Sulphur Springs
West Virginia 24986

Mr. Paul Sturkey, Class of 1980
Chef/Owner
Pigall's Cafe
127 West 4th Street
Cincinnati, Ohio 45202

Mr. John Twichell, Class of 1986
Pastry Chef
The Trellis Restaurant
403 Duke of Gloucester Street
Williamsburg, Virginia 23185

Mr. Carl Walker, Class of 1981
Executive Chef
Brennan's
3300 Smith Street
Houston, Texas 77006

Mr. Joseph Weissenberg, Class of 1958
Senior Chef-Instructor
The Culinary Institute of America
433 Albany Post Road
Hyde Park, New York 12538-1499

Mr. Jasper White, Class of 1976
Chef/Owner
Restaurant Jasper
240 Commercial Street
Boston, Massachusetts 02109

Mr. Alan Zeman, Class of 1981
Executive Chef
Sheraton El Conquistador Resort
10000 North Oracle Road
Tucson, Arizona 85715

••••••• More Good Food and ••••••• Words from the Burger Meisters

Desaulniers, Marcel. *The Trellis Cookbook*. New York: Weidenfeld & Nicolson, 1988.

———. *Death by Chocolate: The Last Word on a Consuming Passion*. New York: Rizzoli International Publications, 1992.

———. *The Trellis Cookbook*. Expanded edition. New York: Simon and Schuster, Fireside Paperbacks, 1992.

Fearing, Dean. *The Mansion on Turtle Creek Cookbook*. New York: Weidenfeld and Nicolson, 1987.

———. *Dean Fearing's Southwest Cuisine: Blending Asia and the Americas*. New York: Grove Weidenfeld, 1990.

Garvin, Kevin. *Seasoned in Texas*. Dallas: Taylor Publishing Company, 1992.

Lang, Jenifer. *Tastings: The Best from Ketchup to Caviar*. New York: Crown Publishers, 1986.

———. *Jenifer Lang Cooks for Kids*. New York: Crown Publishers, Harmony Books, 1991.

Leader, Daniel. *Bread Alone*. New York: William Morrow and Company, 1993.

Routhier, Nicole. *Foods of Vietnam*. New York: Stewart, Tabori & Chang, 1989.

———. *Cooking Under Wraps*. New York: William Morrow and Company, 1993.

Schlesinger, Chris. *The Thrill of the Grill*. New York: William Morrow and Company, 1990.

White, Jasper. *Jasper White's Cooking from New England*. New York: Harper and Row Publishers, 1989.

Index